Praise for

THE DEALERSHIP MANIFESTO

"This book is not theory or fluff—it's a practical playbook built from the real-world experience of running high-performing dealerships. Every chapter delivers clear strategies and actionable steps to increase sales, coach your team, and turn customer experience into the ultimate growth engine."

—**SHANNON SUSKO, founder of Metronomics and bestselling author of *3HAG Way* and *Metronomics***

"As someone who has dedicated his career to building automotive organizations rooted in excellence, I find *The Dealership Manifesto* to be a vital resource for our industry. Bill Napolitano has captured what so many leaders struggle with; how to move from knowing to doing, and from reacting to leading. This book is more than a manual. It is a blueprint for disciplined growth, cultural alignment, and lasting success. Whether you are just beginning your leadership journey or looking to elevate your organization to the next level, this work offers the clarity, tools, and coaching mindset that will help you get there. I strongly recommend it to anyone who values purpose-driven performance and people-first leadership."

—**MARIO MURGADO, President & CEO, Murgado Automotive Group, Inc.**

"*The Dealership Manifesto* delivers a comprehensive roadmap for modern retailing success by offering real-world strategies that align with challenges and opportunities presented every day in auto dealerships."

—SARAH FRYXELL, President, Connecticut Automotive Retailers Association

"With years of experience in coaching and consulting in the dealership community, Bill's guidance in Leadership Mindset and structuring Leadership to Scale are jewels in *The Dealership Manifesto* worthy of any Dealer Ownership Group to tune into and discuss… it will challenge historical, traditional thinking (Mindset), which is how companies break out into new levels of growth, cultural transformation and profitability. The Dealership Manifesto is not just based on Bill's experience, but on many enduring principles of companies that transition from "Good to Great" (with a node to Jim Collins' great work)."

—KEITH CUPP, President and CEO, Gravitas Impact Premium Coaches

"Bill is an insightful advisor with a deep understand of operations and the importance of soft skills needed in the sales and sales management process."

—RAY LOFSTROM, Chief Financial Officer, 24 Auto Group

"Reading this book, I couldn't help but look back and remember how I lived it firsthand—with a group of managers growing a business to 10x its year one size. We "had no time" to train, strategically plan, or do anything but keep our fingers crossed that it would all work out. Until Bill came along, that is. Change is never easy, but if you want to make it in the long run, you need a roadmap for systems, processes, and culture that will keep you aligned and moving forward."

—**SEAN MULLIN**, Co-Owner/General Manager, Souhegan Valley Motorsports

"While this book is particularly addressed to the auto dealership leaders, anyone who wants to run a higher performing business should put this one on their list to read. Here's the map to increased revenues, higher profits, and an enjoyable place to both work as an employee and do business with as a customer. Real world, not theory, how refreshing!"

—**JACK DALY, CEO** Coach, World-Renowned Speaker and Bestselling Author

"People may come and go, but process is forever. Bill has helped dealerships with his 8-Step Roadmap for years, and he understands what works!"

—**GARY DUNCAN**, Owner/Dealer Principal **Duncan Imports & Classics**

"Having worked with Bill for years, I can attest to his deep expertise in dealership operations and his remarkable insight into people. This book captures that knowledge, offering a vital roadmap for anyone in the industry. His experience shows that while many leaders rely on gut instincts or just react to the day, long-term success comes from being strategic, developing leaders, and fostering a strong culture."

—**JOHN LYON, General Manager/ Co-owner, Wilkins Harley Davidson**

"This book is both timely and vital. It addresses the real-world challenges dealership leaders are grappling with and offers a structured, insightful path to shift from gut-driven decisions to purposeful leadership. *The Dealership Manifesto* goes beyond advice—it's a practical leadership resource that can strengthen, elevate, and unify our industry."

—**ED KARDON, Owner/Executive Manager, 24 Auto Group**

THE DEALERSHIP MANIFESTO

THE 8-STEP ROADMAP
TO INDUSTRY-LEADING PROFITABILITY

BILL NAPOLITANO

COPYRIGHT © 2025 BILL NAPOLITANO
All rights reserved.

THE DEALERSHIP MANIFESTO
The 8-Step Roadmap to Industry-Leading Profitability

First Edition

ISBN   978-1-962341-78-3   *Hardcover*
       978-1-962341-77-6   *Paperback*
       978-1-962341-79-0   *Ebook*

To my clients, whose commitment to excellence in serving the retail buying public—whether through advancing transportation solutions, enriching boating experiences, or fostering freedom in the powersports industry—continues to set the standard for innovation and leadership. Your drive and determination have been both the foundation and the inspiration for this work.

A special and heartfelt dedication to my family: my wife, Roseann, and my children, Lisa, Billy, and Michael. Your patience, love, and encouragement have been my constant source of strength. You remind me of what matters most, and your unwavering support has made every step of this journey both possible and worthwhile. You are my greatest source of strength and the true measure of my success.

CONTENTS

INTRODUCTION 1

One	ROADMAP STEP 1: LEADERSHIP	17
Two	ROADMAP STEP 2: STRATEGY	37
Three	ROADMAP STEP 3: RELATIONSHIPS	57
Four	ROADMAP STEP 4: FINANCES	87
Five	ROADMAP STEP 5: SYSTEMS	109
Six	ROADMAP STEP 6: OPERATIONS	133
Seven	ROADMAP STEP 7: REVENUE	157
Eight	ROADMAP STEP 8: MARKETING	173
Nine	COACHING THROUGHOUT THE ORGANIZATION	193

CONCLUSION 215

INTRODUCTION

"We just do things our own way. It works for us."

This was the *last* thing Greg Martin, the new CEO of the recently-purchased Jim Kennis Automotive Group, wanted to hear from his dealership GMs—and it was the fourth time he'd heard it in the last hour.

Jim Kennis Automotive was a dealership group that had a dozen locations across New England. It was the business to beat when it came to vehicle sales; smaller dealerships were constantly in competition, and seasoned sales and service workers wanted to work there over anywhere else. The company's patriarch, Jim Kennis, had announced with fanfare the previous year that he was finally retiring. After a long sale process, the PE firm Greg worked with succeeded in purchasing Jim Kennis Automotive. When Greg was approached to be the new CEO, he jumped at the chance to head up the legendary company and lead it into its new era.

His first step had been to call together all the dealership GMs for a kickoff discussion on the state of the company. And less than a half hour in, Greg wasn't just confused—he was downright *worried*.

Greg had spent his career cleaning up and scaling businesses. He knew what good operations looked like. The overarching trait of any great company was *alignment*. All the different parts of the company needed to be working together like one.

At the kickoff meeting, all the GMs were polite, upbeat—but when they started describing how their stores operated, it was like listening to eight completely different companies.

One GM talked about their own custom finance process. Another mentioned they didn't really follow the same sales tracking system as the other stores. One even laughed and said, "We just figure it out as we go; every day is different."

Greg forced a smile, but his stomach sank. There was no system. No standard. No clear definition of what "good" looked like across the group.

Later that afternoon, back in his office, he scribbled two questions across a yellow legal pad:

1. Do we have the right people in the right roles?
2. What is our strategy?

It wasn't that the stores were broken. Most were profitable. But Greg could see it already—profit without consistency is a ticking clock. If every store was building its own version of success, there would be no way to scale. There would certainly be no way to move a manager from one location to another without disrupting everything. And there would be no way to know if one store's success was replicable, or just a fluke.

INTRODUCTION

The deeper Greg looked, the more he saw the same pattern: Jim Kennis had prided himself on empowering his GMs to "run your store how you want." It sounded good. It felt entrepreneurial. But the result was a patchwork of processes, tools, and cultures. The group had drifted apart without even realizing it.

They needed a shared operating rhythm and strategy, a way to define excellence and actually live it out across every store. Jim Kennis Automotive wasn't a group of stores anymore. It was one company, and Greg intended to create one strategy that aligned all the stores into one smoothly operating profit machine.

He knew that unraveling the old ways and instituting new processes would be a huge undertaking, and a tough sell to a bunch of territorial GMs who were proud of (and maybe had a little bit of ego about) their own unique way of doing things. To get everyone aligned, Greg knew he'd need help.

That's when he called me.

DRIVING TOWARD STRATEGIC ALIGNMENT

Over the past several years, I've had the privilege of working with dealership groups across the country—automotive, powersports, and marine. Some were just getting off the ground; others had been around for generations. Some had shiny new buildings and tech, and others, not so much. But no matter how different they looked on the outside, they all wrestled with the same set of challenges on the inside.

There was an overall lack of discipline; everyone, from sales to service and in between, did things "their own way". There was no standard execution system. Leadership suffered from serious gaps in skill and experience. And as a result of all of these issues, employee turnover was through the roof.

Even if a store was profitable, there was a creeping sense that they could be doing *so much better*.

If that sounds familiar, this book is for you.

As a longtime veteran of the dealership industry, I coach dealerships not just to grow, but to grow in a way that's disciplined, sustainable, and deeply rooted in operational excellence. The approach I take has helped my clients cross into 10x EBITDA territory and stay there. Along the way, I've learned that the biggest problems aren't usually about marketing or inventory. They're about *people*. More specifically, the systems (or lack of them) that either support your people or send them straight out the door.

Let me say this clearly: you don't have a *hiring* problem. You have a *retention* problem.

And retention issues are almost always symptoms of three core gaps:

1. A lack of discipline
2. A lack of a strong, repeatable execution system
3. Gaps in leadership at every level

INTRODUCTION

When these go unchecked, chaos creeps in. You lose good people. Your managers feel overwhelmed. Everyone ends up reacting to the day instead of leading it. And when that becomes the norm, growth slows—or worse, stalls completely.

The good news is this can be fixed. Not with a flavor-of-the-month initiative or a one-day workshop, but with a connected system—a way of running your business that creates alignment, drives results, and actually gets people excited to come to work.

That's what this book is all about.

In this book, you'll learn the exact 8-step roadmap I use with high-performing dealerships across the auto, powersports, and marine industries. It's designed to help you lead better, plan smarter, and execute more consistently. It's a set of practical tools and systems you can use to create a culture of excellence that lasts.

1. Step 1: Leadership
2. Step 2: Strategy
3. Step 3: Relationships
4. Step 4: Finances
5. Step 5: Systems
6. Step 6: Operations
7. Step 7: Revenue
8. Step 8: Marketing

The first three steps of the 8-Step Roadmap—Leadership, Strategy, and Relationships—may seem like "soft skills" that aren't as immediately important as the nuts-and-bolts content of the rest of the book, but I want to caution you *not* to skip ahead. Leadership, Strategy and Relationships form the building blocks of the most crucial foundation for the longevity and scalability of your business: culture. If you skip those chapters, you might as well put this book down and not read it! Each step of the Roadmap is a critical part of your journey.

No matter where you're starting from—whether you're taking over a group that's lost its edge or trying to build something great from the ground up—I believe this book can help you get there.

FROM PASSENGER TO DRIVER

Have you ever felt like you're just a passenger in your own business—along for the ride, and just reacting to roadblocks as they happen?

I would bet the house that the reason for this is a lack of strategic clarity.

It's something I see in most of the dealerships I work with: a lot of dealerships don't really *have* a clear strategy. Leaders are often doing their best to figure things out as they go, relying on gut instincts and past experience to get through the day. It's not that they don't care; far from it. They care tremendously, and take great pride in making their stores profitable. It's just that no one ever really taught them how to lead strategically.

That's not surprising when you look at how most people get

INTRODUCTION

into this business.

Some folks start their dealership careers with a background in leadership or formal business training, but that's not incredibly common. Most actually begin in sales—some because they love cars or boats or bikes, others because the paycheck looked promising. And while a lot of them work hard, build strong habits, and learn to sell like pros, they don't necessarily get exposed to the bigger-picture stuff: strategic planning, coaching, or how to lead a growing team.

Fast forward a few years, and those same people might be running a store. They're managing dozens of employees, dealing with inventory, handling customer issues—and doing it all without much support or a clear roadmap. It's no wonder things start to feel reactive and a little chaotic.

Part of the issue is the constant pressure to hit the numbers. Every month, every quarter, sales targets rule the day. And while meeting those goals is obviously important, that laser-focus on short-term results can start to edge out the things that actually help a dealership grow. Things like leadership development, team building, and long-term planning, which are all aspects of a strong organizational culture (a key step on the 8-Step Roadmap you'll learn in this book).

When everything is about hitting today's number, no one has the time or energy to step back and ask, *Where are we actually going?*

What ends up happening is a lot of firefighting. Decisions are made in the moment, based on what just happened, instead of what should happen next. Leaders get stuck in survival mode. And the business suffers. In fact, at the time I'm writing this book, dealerships are facing especially high uncertainty; looming tariffs, customer fears, and everyone is tightening their belts. It's never been more important to buckle down on your systems, people, culture, and processes.

The truth is, if a dealership wants to thrive, not just survive, it has to start thinking differently. It needs leaders who are willing to zoom out and look at the whole picture. People who are serious about learning, coaching their teams, and creating a culture where growth is possible.

The dealerships that succeed long-term aren't just great at selling. They're great at leading. They have a fantastic culture that you can feel when you walk in the door. They build systems, develop talent, and customer relationships, and stay focused on where they're going, not just what they sold last week. They're *driving* the business, not just along for the ride.

You can absolutely build that kind of dealership. This book will show you how.

BUILDING DEALERSHIPS BETTER

I've been in the automotive business in one way or another for most of my life. My first job out of college was selling cars at

INTRODUCTION

a Chevrolet dealership. I didn't last long in that role, but not because I didn't care—I just asked too many questions. At one point I asked, "How do we even know what we sold last month?" and no one had an answer. That's how I accidentally became the assistant sales manager, mostly keeping records that didn't exist until I created them.

That thread carried through the next chapters of my career. I moved from retail into the manufacturer side, working first for Chrysler and then General Motors as a district sales manager. I spent years supporting dealers, helping them with inventory, allocations, and strategy. It was fast-paced, exciting—and full of constant transfers. When the corporate machine told me I'd be moving to northern Maine in the dead of winter, I politely declined.

For a few years, I dove back into retail. I became the GM of a Chevrolet dealership in Boston, but only ran that store for a short period—within a matter of months, the dealer purchased three other stores, and I found myself promoted to the VP of Sales for the newly expanded group. But then, after a couple of years, I came to a realization: I didn't want to manage dealerships anymore.

Instead, I wanted to help people build and lead dealerships better. That's when I found coaching. I joined a leadership development organization in 1998, and I've been doing that work ever since.

What I love most about coaching leaders at dealerships isn't fixing broken processes or driving up sales; it's watching people grow into who they're capable of becoming. There's something deeply rewarding about helping a leader see their own potential, maybe for the first time, and giving them the tools and space to chase it. I ask a lot of questions—sometimes uncomfortable ones—not because I have all the answers, but because I believe they do. They just haven't been asked the right way yet.

When a leader starts thinking differently, seeing new connections, gaining confidence, it's like watching a lightbulb go on.

That moment is why I coach. It's also why I wrote this book.

THE LEADERSHIP MINDSET SHIFT

In nearly every dealership I've worked with, there's a consistent theme that shows up early in the conversation: people are looking for a quick fix. And in many cases, they're also looking for a *cheap* one.

That's not a criticism. It's just the reality of an industry where leaders are constantly under pressure, chasing the next target, and trying to stay ahead of competitors. When you're caught up in the day-to-day chaos, the idea of investing in long-term leadership or strategic development can feel like a luxury you simply can't afford. But it's exactly that mindset that keeps so many dealerships stuck in reactive mode.

Recently, I spoke at two state association conferences where this topic came up again and again. The enthusiastic audience response

INTRODUCTION

wasn't about me being a particularly impressive speaker, I assure you. It was about the message striking a nerve. What I spoke about wasn't new. It was just framed in a way that helped people finally *see* the problem clearly.

Here's what I shared: *many dealership leaders are measuring success in a way that doesn't reflect what's really going on.*

They might be proud to be top performers in a peer group, but at the same time, they're losing money month over month. And underneath that disconnect is a deeper issue: a lack of attention to the cost of turnover and the cost of poor leadership development.

Let me give you an example. Imagine you promote a talented salesperson to a sales manager role—but you don't train or develop her for that position. It happens all the time. And I want to be clear: I don't blame the managers. Most of them are trying their best. They're looking around and thinking, *I guess I'll just do what the last guy did.* The problem is, they also saw the last guy get fired. So now we're repeating a cycle that nobody is proud of and nobody knows how to break.

What really opens people's eyes is when I ask this question: *How much gross profit do you think a manager generates in a month?* And then I ask them to do the math—multiply that number by twelve. More often than not, we're talking about an individual responsible for producing seven figures in annual gross profit. Not revenue—gross profit.

Then I ask, *How much are you investing in that person's develop-*

ment?

It's almost never proportional. People are shocked when they realize they'll spend $5,000 or $10,000 on a single week of training and expect it to completely transform a leader responsible for driving a million dollars in gross profit. Even worse, they'll pour hundreds of thousands of dollars into advertising that doesn't move the needle, while leadership development sits on the back burner.

When I lay that out, the room usually goes quiet. Because for many of them, it's the first time they've really connected those dots.

There's another layer to this too. Everyone is so focused on the numbers, and the pressure is constant. I recently described it to a group as being like the Acela train speeding up and down the East Coast at 160 miles per hour. It's fast. It's relentless. And nobody feels like they can slow down long enough to train or coach anyone properly.

But if they did—if they slowed the train just a bit to develop their people—they'd actually gain time in the long run. They'd have fewer customer complaints, less rework, fewer frustrations, and better results.

The real obstacle here isn't time. It's mindset. And what dealerships need is a mindset shift, a fundamental change in how leaders think about strategy, leadership, and growth.

That shift is what this book is about.

Many leaders I've worked with don't actually know what strategy is, let alone how to build one for their business that will drive

INTRODUCTION

real results. This book will help you understand what strategy really means and why it matters. From there, the goal is to guide you through developing a real, intentional, and most importantly, *differentiated* strategy.

Strategy starts at the top. That's also where the bottleneck is. In fact, in every organization I've ever worked with, the bottleneck is always the same—it's at the top. (Just like a bottle. No surprise there.)

That's why the dealer principal has to lead the charge. They need to define the strategy of the business, validate it with their team, and make sure it's clearly communicated across the entire organization. Not just once. Continuously. And that strategy has to stand out—it can't be generic. It needs to set the business apart and give people a reason to rally behind it.

This isn't about throwing money at the problem or checking a box with a one-day seminar. It's about making leadership and strategy part of the way you run the business, every single day.

LET'S DIVE IN

Not long ago, I was working with a dealer who was visibly proud of his position in a well-known performance group. He told me he ranked number one or two out of about twenty peers. From his perspective, that was the mark of success.

But then I asked him a simple question: "How did your store

actually do last month?"

He paused and said, almost as an afterthought, "Well... we did have a negative net profit."

That moment perfectly captures why this book exists.

There's a strange and dangerous paradox in the dealership world. Leaders are often measuring themselves against benchmarks that don't actually reflect the health of their business. Being top of your peer group might feel like a win, but if your store is bleeding cash, what's the point?

Too many dealers are chasing a sense of success without understanding what's really driving it—or hurting it.

And the truth is, the numbers tell a sobering story. Margins are razor thin. At any given moment, most stores are just a couple of decisions or missteps away from going over the edge financially.

It doesn't have to be this way.

The reason for writing this book is simple: I believe there's a better way to run a dealership. A smarter, more disciplined way that doesn't rely on guesswork, gut instinct, or outdated habits. What leaders in this industry need isn't another motivational talk or an isolated best practice. They need a full, proven system—a process that brings stability, growth, and ultimately, wealth.

That's what the 8-Step Roadmap you'll learn in this book is about.

This book is for the leaders who are tired of just getting by, tired of celebrating surface-level wins while quietly dealing with deep

INTRODUCTION

operational pain. It's for those who want to know with certainty that their business is not just surviving, but actually thriving.

So why would someone pick up this book? Why would they invest the time to read it or consider bringing in a coach like me?

Because they want something solid. They want to stop guessing. They want a dealership that isn't on the edge of a cliff.

They're ready for a real process—one that works.

That's what we're going to dive into together. Let's go.

CHAPTER ONE

ROADMAP STEP 1: LEADERSHIP

When I got the call from Greg Martin to step in and help with Jim Kennis Automotive, I was floored. This was a massive opportunity.

For more than five decades, Jim Kennis Automotive had stood as the gold standard in the New England area. Customers knew it. Vendors respected it. Competitors watched it. And when the news broke that Jim Kennis was retiring, and had sold the business to a private equity firm, the industry took notice.

This included me. I was *very* interested to see if JKA would go through any organizational changes, staffing changes, or brand shifts.

In fact, when Greg got in touch with me, I assumed he wanted help with what should have been a smooth transition. After all, JKA stores were everywhere, and doing great by all appearances.

"We've got a big problem," he told me before I flew out to meet with the GMs. "This isn't a company; this is a collection of a dozen different companies with no clear vision."

Some stores looked strong on the surface—impressive facilities, decent numbers, solid reputations—but when Greg dug a little deeper, he found the cracks. A few locations were quietly underperforming. Customer satisfaction was inconsistent. Some general managers lacked clear direction. None of them seemed to understand that they were part of a team, not an individual business. These stores weren't thriving so much as they were coasting on the Kennis name.

It's a situation that's more common than most people realize.

When you're looking at the success of an organization, it's easy to focus on the whole and miss the parts. Think of it like a chain-link fence. From a distance, it might look sturdy and secure. But if you walk along it and inspect each link, you'll often find weak spots. In a group like Jim Kennis Automotive, the brand may shine, but there are always a few locations dragging the rest down.

This happens for a number of reasons. Sometimes stores have been bought and sold multiple times. Sometimes legacy leadership remains in place too long. Other times, newer hires are dropped into roles without enough support or oversight. And while the group, overall, may look strong, there are often "holes in the boat" that go unnoticed until they start affecting the bottom line.

Successful companies avoid this issue by investing in the piece of the puzzle with by far the biggest impact: leadership.

They plan ahead. They take a hard look at their leadership pipeline—inside and outside the family. They ask, *Who is ready? Who*

CHAPTER ONE

isn't? And what would it take to get them there?

I've worked with groups where these conversations happen far too late, and it seemed like JKA would be no different. No one could deny that Jim Kennis had built something extraordinary. But even in a group as storied as his, there were gaps. Stores that didn't quite measure up. Leaders who weren't aligned. Processes that had started to drift.

No matter how big your group, how respected your name, or how successful you've been—success comes down to *leadership*. Not just at the top, but in every location. At the end of the day, it's not the name on the sign that matters most. It's what's happening behind the doors.

SCALING LEADERSHIP

There's something that happens when a dealership or a dealership group grows. From the outside looking in, it often appears polished and successful. The branding is consistent, the signage is sharp, and the footprint suggests something well-run and trustworthy. But when you peel back the layers, a different story often starts to emerge.

Yes, the group may look unified. But inside, it's usually a collection of different operations—each with its own issues, its own processes, and, most importantly, its own interpretation of leadership.

Leadership exists in every corner of the dealership: store managers, department heads, service advisors, even senior technicians guiding more junior team members. Everyone who influences direction, behavior, and performance is a leader in some way. And in multi-store organizations, the strength—or weakness—of that leadership plays out store by store.

Now, to be fair, many large groups try to centralize things as they scale. Some create management companies to oversee daily operations across stores. Others build regional hubs or central offices. In theory, this approach makes sense. For example, instead of having eight different office managers at eight different stores, they might consolidate the function. Maybe four people handle billing across the entire group. Maybe there's one CFO, a few controllers that serve multiple stores, and specialized office staff instead of a full admin team at every single location.

This kind of shared service model can reduce overhead and increase efficiency. But it also requires something most groups struggle to maintain: *alignment*.

That's where things start to fall apart.

One of the most damaging things a dealer principal can say—usually with the best of intentions—is, "It's your store. Run it the way you want." That's how Jim Kennis had trained his managers, and they interpreted it as full autonomy. Once that door is open, it doesn't take long before every GM is building their own version of what a store should look like.

The same is true for leaders inside a single dealership, like de-

CHAPTER ONE

partment heads. If all the departments in your dealership don't speak the same language, pretty soon things will drift towards chaos.

Different sales processes. Different customer follow-up routines. Different service standards. Different leadership behaviors.

Now, are there times when store leaders and department leaders need flexibility? Absolutely. Different markets, demographics, and store sizes will call for some degree of customization. Different departments have different missions, rhythms, and needs. But that's not the same as every leader doing everything their own way. When systems aren't aligned, when leadership expectations vary, and when culture is left to chance, you don't have much of a company anymore.

Processes become fragmented. Training becomes harder. Moving people between locations or departments becomes almost impossible. Culture isn't reinforced, and as a result, it gets rewritten every day.

All of this leads to the place no CEO or leader wants to find themselves: the company is stagnating and incredibly difficult to scale.

The goal in any leadership group, whether it's across stores or within one location, should be simple: create consistency in process, in culture, and in expectations. That doesn't mean stifling creativity or micromanaging. It means giving your people the structure they need to operate effectively, lead clearly, and deliver the kind of experience your brand promises.

Without that consistency, even the most successful-looking group or dealership will struggle under the weight of its own disorganization.

Leadership must be intentional. Culture must be reinforced. And processes must be aligned.

Otherwise, you'll keep hearing that dreaded phrase over and over again: "That's not how we do it at our store."

DO WE HAVE THE RIGHT PEOPLE?

The first question Greg Martin had written down after his first day meeting with the GMs was a huge red flag that something was not right within the company.

Do we have the right people?

Now, in a traditional business, this is a question the CEO would consistently check in on and stay on top of. But in Greg's case, coming into the dealership world, he had looked around the room at a group of managers who brought with them a huge variety of backgrounds, experience levels, and leadership styles. It didn't seem like hiring and developing these leaders had been done with a whole lot of thought or planning.

This didn't surprise me. If there's one pattern I've seen time and again in dealerships, it's that people end up in leadership roles not necessarily because they're the best equipped, but because they

CHAPTER ONE

were *there*.

Maybe they had some industry experience. Maybe they were successful in a different role—say, sales or service—and got promoted. But once in the new position, it became clear they didn't actually have the tools to lead. Not in a sustainable, strategic way. And to be fair, it's not their fault. Most people working in dealerships didn't grow up dreaming of it. They didn't study for it. They didn't train to become leaders in this space.

They backed into it.

What usually happens is someone hears there's money to be made in sales. They take the job. And because the commission checks come quickly, there's not a lot of motivation to slow down and learn the bigger picture—how the business actually works, how to coach people, or how to lead with intention.

So they keep moving up. And before long, you have people making big decisions about operations, staffing, customer experience, and growth without the training or strategy to do it well.

Most dealership leaders don't have a clear strategic intent. They don't know what that means, let alone how to build it. Some might claim to have a strategy, but if you press a little, what you find is closer to a set of habits or instincts.

"Wing it" is not a strategy—but you'd be surprised to hear how often the dealerships I work with run solely on the leader's instincts. When a business is built around instinct alone, it creates confusion, misalignment, and eventually stagnation.

These aren't bad people. They're not lazy or careless. They're just overwhelmed.

Because here's what else is true: *everyone's too busy*. Or, more accurately, everyone *thinks* they're too busy, because they don't have the right systems in place to support efficient operations.

Dealerships run fast. The pressure to hit the numbers every month is unrelenting. That focus—"Just make the numbers"—dominates everything. Coaching falls to the bottom of the list. Leadership development gets sidelined. Strategy becomes something you "get to" later, if ever.

When problems do pop up, most leaders go looking for a fast, cheap fix. It might work for a little while, but eventually the same problems will come back again and again like a weed.

And that's why so many of the same issues keep repeating. The wrong people are in the wrong roles. Stores are reacting instead of leading. Leaders are struggling not because they don't care, but because they've never been shown another way.

The good news is there *is* another way to lead. It's not flashy, but it works. And it starts with shifting the mindset—from chasing short-term results to building long-term strength. From reacting to each day to leading with intention. That's what the chapters ahead will walk through. Not theory, but practical steps for building real leadership inside your dealership from the ground up.

CHAPTER ONE

THE LEADERSHIP ACTION PLAN

Once you get this done, you might ask yourself Greg's question, and the answer is "no". That's when you need to have tough conversations and drop the wrong leaders to get the right leaders in place.

So, how do you know if you have the right people in leadership? The following questions should be answered for each person you're evaluating:

1. Do they have the **desire to excel?**
2. Do they have the **willingness to do what it takes?**
3. Do they have the **discipline to execute?**

THE DESIRE TO EXCEL

One of the core truths about leadership is that excellence isn't something you stumble into. It's something you have to pursue intentionally, with a fire that doesn't easily burn out.

Excellence, in this context, isn't about chasing perfection. It's about consistently getting the outcomes you're aiming for. In my world, those outcomes are not vague or abstract. They're very clear, very measurable. We're talking about bottom-line results: revenue, profitability, return on investment. Without a strong return, the dealership simply can't grow. It's that black and white.

But here's the deeper layer that matters even more: it's not enough to want success *casually*. There needs to be an *ongoing* desire to excel. Real desire to excel doesn't flicker with every obstacle. It burns steadily, even when things get hard.

Sometimes it shows up as a burning desire, the kind of drive where leaders and teams aren't just *hoping* to succeed; they *expect* to. This is what you're looking for in the people you have in leadership.

- They set clear goals, and when they fall short, they don't shrug it off.
- They take success and failure personally.
- They care deeply about the result, not out of ego, but out of pride and commitment to what they're building.

You can often see it in the way people react when things don't go as planned. Someone with a burning desire to excel will get frustrated when the ball gets dropped, but not in a blaming, destructive way. It's a productive frustration. It's the voice inside that says, "This matters too much to let it slide."

It keeps teams from settling for mediocrity. It creates an environment where learning, growth, and accountability aren't just buzzwords, but everyday realities.

And most importantly, it gives the organization resilience. Because setbacks will happen. Challenges are guaranteed. But a team with a true desire to excel doesn't crumble when things get tough. They regroup, refocus, and keep moving forward.

That kind of energy changes everything. If the leaders at a

CHAPTER ONE

dealership model this mindset, you'll see it show up in their team members. It will spread throughout the whole dealership until it's a deep-rooted part of the culture.

THE WILLINGNESS TO DO WHAT IT TAKES

If the desire to excel is the first step toward meaningful success, the second step is just as critical: the willingness to do what it takes, and to learn what needs to be learned.

It sounds simple on the surface. Most people would say they're willing to work hard or put in extra effort when needed. But true willingness goes deeper than that. To be willing to do what it takes, you need to be okay with stepping outside your comfort zone, admitting when you don't know something, and being open enough to grow, even when growth feels hard or uncomfortable.

Let's face it: in this industry, we're often dealing with a lot of big egos. I'm not saying that as a good thing or a bad thing; it's just a fact. Ego is good when it means you take pride in your work. Where ego can kill leadership, though, is when it turns into arrogance. A leader who is set in their ways, who thinks they know everything and won't adjust to new information or learn new skills, has no place in leadership. If you're seeing that tendency in any of your people, you might need to make changes.

Real willingness to do what it takes means recognizing that past success doesn't guarantee future results. What worked before may not work tomorrow. The market shifts. Customer expectations change. Technology evolves.

The leaders and teams who thrive are the ones who stay curious. They keep asking, "What do I need to know that I don't know yet?"

It also means being ready to do the unglamorous work. Sometimes learning what needs to be learned means sitting through the tough meetings, making the difficult phone calls, or practicing the basics again and again until they become second nature. It's not always exciting or celebrated, but it's the kind of steady, committed work that builds a strong foundation for lasting success.

The willingness to do what it takes also requires humility. It's easy to fall into the trap of thinking, "I've been doing this for years. I know enough." But the truth is, real leadership means being a lifelong learner. It means choosing growth over comfort. It means being just as committed to improving yourself as you are to improving your business.

Learning isn't a one-time event. It's not something you check off a list after attending a workshop or reading a book; it's a daily choice. It's showing up each morning with the mindset that says, "Today, I'm willing to learn something new. I'm willing to get a little better." The best leaders make learning into a daily routine and ritual.

When leaders embrace that kind of willingness, it sets the tone for the entire organization. It gives permission for others to be learners too. It creates a culture where growth isn't only expected but supported. Over time, it builds an environment where excellence isn't an accident. It's the natural outcome of people who are constantly stretching, adapting, and becoming the best version of themselves.

THE DISCIPLINE TO EXECUTE

Discipline often gets a bad reputation. It sounds rigid and exhausting, and like something that requires a lot of willpower (and that's true; it does!).

But it's a non-negotiable, and it's the third trait you need to evaluate in the people you have in leadership.

When it comes to discipline, the key is routine. Part of any strong strategy is creating routines that embed that strategy into daily life. Routines are what set us free. They take the guesswork out of important tasks. They allow us to operate with clarity and confidence, even when the pressure's on.

Every dealership you walk into has routines. There are things that happen automatically, no matter what kind of day they're having. Maybe it's how inventory's checked, how customer calls are handled, or how repair orders are processed.

The important thing to remember is: *your dealership's current routines are producing your dealership's current outcomes.*

Not seeing the outcomes you want? Take a look at the routines of each department. You might find that they need tweaking or updating, and that's a normal factor in organizational management.

But if you find that a department has lax routines, or *no* real routines, that's a leadership issue. The leader isn't modeling the discipline to execute.

You may have already experienced pushback when trying to get people to change up their routines to improve their outcomes. Leaders and teams will say, "I don't have time to change that." Sales are down, so they can't afford to pull people off the showroom floor. Managers feel like they can't spare a single moment because they're already behind pace for the month.

It's understandable. When the pressure's mounting, the instinct is to speed up, to do more of what you're already doing. But that's the old mindset and routine, and the old mindset and routine is what created the current results.

Here's the question you need to ask any leader who pushes back on changing up their routines:

"How's that working for you?"

The truth, more often than not, is that it *isn't* working. And if something isn't working, why in the world would you keep doing it?

Changing routines requires slowing down long enough to see what needs to change. It demands trust that building better habits today will create better results tomorrow. Leaders with the discipline to execute understand this and will take the time to establish routines that produce results.

CHAPTER ONE

RIGHT PEOPLE, RIGHT STRATEGY

With the Leadership Action Plan you just read, you should be able to take a hard look at the people you've got in leadership roles and answer the crucial question: "Do we have the right people?"

You might find that for many of them, the answer is *yes*. (Fantastic!)

You might find that for some of them, the answer is *yes, but in the wrong seat*. That's great. Right person, wrong seat is a fixable problem. If they have the three traits you're looking for, you're going to be able to train them up to either be right for the role they're in, or move to another role in the organization they're better suited for. (Providing that they want to move to that role, of course. It's not always so simple, and you should prepare yourself to lose good people who may not want to leave their current role and go into a role they're better suited for. Often, they just can't picture themselves there.)

But you might find that for a few people (hopefully very few), the answer is *no*. If this is the case, you need to make quick changes.

I've worked with so many dealerships where hard conversations are being avoided. No one wants to step on anyone's toes or kick off conflict. Bad leaders are allowed to stay in their roles far longer than they should. They create a culture in their team that eventually spreads through the whole organization.

With the high speed and low margin of dealership business, you can't afford to have the wrong people in leadership. You need to get the right people in the right roles as quickly as possible so that you can focus on what will really accelerate the dealership's growth and success: *strategy*.

It's impossible to create and execute on strategy if you don't have alignment among your leaders. It also won't be possible to execute on the rest of the 8-Step Roadmap until you have the right people in place. That's why this chapter came first, and that's where you need to put your focus.

Everything in the dealership starts with the people who run it. Make sure they're up to the task.

THE WORK IS JUST BEGINNING

My first meeting with JKA took place in a modest training room above one of the flagship stores. Nothing fancy—just a circle of chairs, a whiteboard, and twelve general managers who clearly weren't sure what to make of me.

I stood at the front of the room, hands in my pockets, and said, "Let's start simple. When you think about success at your store—how do you define it?"

There was a long pause.

Then Jeff, a sharp, numbers-driven GM from Rhode Island, spoke up first. "We hit our forecast. We hit our gross. We're suc-

CHAPTER ONE

cessful."

"Alright," I nodded, scribbling on the board. "Forecast and gross."

Angela jumped in next. "I'd say it's our retention. We've had almost zero turnover this year. People like working for us."

"Good. Retention. That matters."

From there, it snowballed. One person talked about CSI scores. Another talked about inventory turns. Someone else mentioned departmental profit margins. Someone else said, "Honestly? If the store feels calm and I'm not putting out fires every hour, that's success."

By the time everyone had spoken, the board was full. I turned around and looked at the words scattered across it—twelve definitions of success, each valid, each totally different.

I smiled. "Okay," I said. "This explains a lot."

Some of them laughed. A few just stared back.

"None of you are wrong," I continued. "But you're not aligned, either. And that's a problem."

Later, I'd meet with each of them one-on-one. I'd sit in their offices, walk their lots, watch how their teams moved and talked and solved problems. Some stores had systems that ran like clockwork. Others ran entirely on personality and hustle.

One of those store visits was with Ben, a longtime GM who looked like he hadn't had a day off in five years. His desk was buried in paperwork. He kept glancing at his phone during our conversation.

"Look," he said, "I know we're messy. But we're making it work."

"Ben," I said gently, "you're making it work. But this whole place falls apart if you take a vacation. That's not a system, it's survival. *Barely*."

He didn't argue.

Over the next few weeks, I worked with the GMs individually and as a group to define their leadership principles and standards.

"What does great look like?" I asked them. "Not at your store. Not in theory. But across this group—what do we all agree matters?"

We debated. We clarified. And slowly, we started to shape something together. A shared definition of excellence. A framework for how we onboard employees. How we treat customers. How we lead teams.

It wasn't quick. It wasn't easy. There were hard conversations, some resistance, and a lot of rewiring or mindsets.

Once we were done, we'd crossed Step 1 off the Roadmap, and the JKA leaders were ready to bring their new direction and alignment back to their stores. To really change how things operated, they'd need to get their whole staff on board.

Changes like that don't come easily in dealerships, where people tend to cling to what works for them and resist anything new. So, in all honesty, the GMs thought they'd tackled the hard part in

CHAPTER ONE

the work we'd already done—but the hard part was just beginning.

Luckily, we were about to move into Step 2 of the 8-Step Roadmap: Strategy. And I was about to introduce them to the most effective tool in their toolbelt to get their staff aligned, focused, and on the same page: the One Page Roadmap.

KEY TAKEAWAYS ON LEADERSHIP

Here are five key takeaways from this chapter:

1. **Leadership alignment is essential for sustainable success.** No matter how respected the brand or how strong individual locations may appear, without unified leadership standards, processes, and culture, a dealership group will struggle to scale and perform consistently.

2. **Every department should operate like its own business—but not in isolation.** While some department-specific flexibility is needed, a "run it how you want" mindset creates fragmented operations and misaligned teams. Each department in the dealership must follow shared leadership principles and expectations.

3. **Leadership roles require more than experience—they require strategic capability.**

Many dealership leaders are promoted based on tenure or past performance, not readiness to lead. Without the desire to excel, willingness to grow, and discipline to execute, they can't drive consistent performance or culture.

4. **You can't afford to keep the wrong people in leadership.** Having the right people in the right seats is non-negotiable. Leaders who lack alignment, capacity, or openness to coaching will drag down culture and growth—and addressing that misalignment is the first step in building an effective organization.

5. **Culture isn't what you say—it's what your leaders model every day.** Defining success, aligning leadership behaviors, and embedding those expectations across all stores is the foundation of dealership transformation. Without this clarity, each location will default to survival mode, and the brand will suffer as a result.

CHAPTER TWO

ROADMAP STEP 2: STRATEGY

Over the course of a few intensive days, the leaders of Jim Kennis Automotive had made incredible progress, and everyone left the session with what felt like great momentum.

I stood in the parking lot afterward watching them head to their cars. There was laughter, handshakes, even a couple of real smiles. We'd laid out a plan that made sense. Even better, the initial resistance of "we do things our way" seemed to have mostly dropped away.

"I don't want to jinx it," Greg said to me as we watched everyone drive away into the late afternoon, "but I think we might be out of the woods."

Three days later, he called me out of the blue. "I knew I shouldn't have jinxed it!" he said.

After the session, Greg had started making the rounds, visiting all the stores in the group. What he found clued him in instantly to much bigger problems we hadn't even begun to deal with yet.

"The feeling in several of the stores was just wrong," he told me.

The tension that had been so apparent at the managers meeting was everywhere, in the snappy way the service desk at one store answered calls, to the way salespeople talked about customers (not to their faces, thankfully). Employees were going through the motions. The managers were reacting and putting out fires, but not leading.

Greg described it perfectly in our call: "It's like we planted new seeds in bad soil."

That's when I knew we had to go back to the beginning.

The next week, I asked Greg to bring all twelve GMs back together. This time, we had to talk about the foundation of the company's culture: Vision. Mission. Values. Purpose.

It was quiet when we started; everyone was probably wondering what we were all doing back together so soon, but instead, I asked a simple question: "What are we building here?"

One of the managers shrugged. "A profitable company."

I nodded. "That's part of it. But what else?" I pulled out a marker and drew four boxes on the whiteboard.

Vision Mission. Values. Purpose.

"This is what we need to nail down next, before we map out our strategy," I explained. "From what Greg has told me, it doesn't feel like the stores all share a common culture that's driving them forward."

Another manager—unsurprisingly, the one from the store Greg had described as having the worst overall energy—looked skeptical as he said, "Sorry, but what does culture have to do with strategy? We're here to make money, not to plan team happy hours."

His question was one I'd heard countless times from other teams I'd coached. *What does culture have to do with strategy?*

As you'll learn in this chapter, *everything*.

WHERE STRATEGY BEGINS

When we talk about strategy in a dealership, it's tempting to jump straight into action.

What are we doing today to sell more cars? How are we marketing our service department? Are we hitting our monthly goals?

Those questions matter, but they are not where true strategy begins.

If we want to build something that lasts, we have to think a level up from actions. We have to step back and ask a bigger, foundational question: What is the unique and differentiating set of activities that will guide decisions across the entire organization?

In other words, what is the company's culture?

Strategy doesn't start with setting monthly targets or running new promotions. Those are tactical moves, and if you only focus on tactics without a clear foundation, you end up reacting to every new challenge instead of leading from the front. Over time, that approach creates confusion, frustration, and inconsistency rather than growth.

Before you worry about the details, like sales scripts, advertising plans, or CRM processes, you have to make sure you've built the right cultural foundation. You have to know who you are as an organization, what you stand for, and how you expect people to think and act when they're representing your brand.

It's easy to get so focused on *doing* things that you forget to ask whether those things you're doing are aligned with who you want to be as a business. But the best organizations that grow sustainably, attract loyal customers, and keep top talent take their culture very seriously. They're crystal clear about their values and expectations, and they build everything else on top of that clarity.

Strategy begins with the following cultural foundation:

1. Vision
2. Mission
3. Values
4. Purpose

In this chapter, you're going to learn how to define that foundation, get everyone aligned and on the same page, and use a powerful strategic tool—the One Page Dealership Roadmap—to build on the foundation and create a top-performing organization.

"CULTURE EATS STRATEGY FOR BREAKFAST"

You may have heard this phrase from Peter Drucker before, and in my experience, it couldn't be more true in the dealership setting. Culture creates the framework for how operations should function. When a dealership takes time to define its culture with intention, it lays the groundwork for everything that follows—from how people lead, to how decisions are made, to how success is defined across the organization.

There are four elements that help shape this cultural foundation from an operational point of view: **vision, mission, values, and purpose.**

Vision is where the organization is headed. It may be five years out, or maybe ten, but it's the destination the team is working toward. It's the long view, the larger impact the business wants to make.

Mission supports that vision by defining how the team will move toward it. This is where the real action starts. It's the structure behind the day-to-day effort. Mission keeps everyone aligned and moving in the same direction, even when they're working in different departments or dealing with different challenges.

Values are the behavioral expectations that hold everything together. They're meant to be active expressions of what matters most inside the business. They show up in employee behaviors, how people treat each other, how leaders respond under pressure, how employees are supported and held accountable, and the experience customers have inside the dealership.

Purpose is the reason the dealership exists in the first place.

Not the financial goals or the market share targets, but the deeper motivation and belief behind the work. This is what gives meaning to long hours and challenging seasons. When people know *why* the business exists, they connect differently, care differently, and lead differently.

Together, vision, mission, values, and purpose become the backbone of how the business operates. They shape priorities, influence communication, and give people the clarity they need to lead well and grow with confidence. When these four elements are clear and aligned, the culture supports and strengthens the operation.

But if they're missing or left undefined, or defined but not taken seriously, people begin to drift. That's when departments start building their own silos, and when leaders start solving problems with short-term tactics instead of long-term conviction. That's also where you get the issues Jim Kennis Automotive was having: every manager rigidly stuck to "doing it our way".

When we start to talk about culture—vision, mission, values, purpose—it's not uncommon for someone to push back. I've heard it many times: "This is a car dealership. We sell cars." The implication is clear: *culture sounds nice, but it doesn't apply here.*

Some leaders have even told me flat out, "Employees are a dime a dozen. We hire, they leave, we hire again." That kind of turnover has been accepted as normal in this industry for so long that it's become part of the dealership story. And I get it—many of these folks came up in environments where people really did come and go constantly. There wasn't a lot of investment in culture, because the expectation was that no one would stay long enough to make it matter.

But when you scratch beneath that surface, the cracks start to show. It's not that people don't care. It's that they've never been taught how to anchor the business to something deeper than transactions. Once they see the connection between culture and performance, things start to shift.

DEFINING YOUR CULTURE

When I work with dealers, CEOs, and leadership teams to talk about shaping the future of a dealership, one of the most important questions I ask is: "What are you trying to build?"

It sounds like a basic starting point, but it's often the question that brings the conversation to a halt. Because much of the time, those leaders don't have a clear answer.

That's not because they aren't smart or experienced. Most of the people I work with have been in this business for a long time; they've done the hard work. They've turned wrenches, written deals, run service departments, and managed teams. Some came up through family businesses, and others bought their way in after years of learning the ropes. They've earned their seat.

But having that kind of history doesn't always mean you've had the time to step back and define what you want the future to look like. For many leaders, especially those who've spent years operating in the thick of the day-to-day, the idea of an "endgame" can feel a little vague. Sometimes it's never been asked before. Sometimes it's been asked in passing, but never answered clearly.

When I sit down with someone and ask directly what their endgame is, things shift. The moment a leader starts to answer that question, they move from *reacting* to *leading*.

I saw this play out clearly with a client I'd worked with for quite a while. We were in the middle of a leadership meeting, reviewing plans and next steps, when I paused and asked him the million-dollar question: "What's your endgame?"

I wanted to know where he was trying to take the business. What was the long-term goal? What was he building toward?

He told me something that surprised me, only because he had never talked about it before. His endgame was to build generational wealth.

That one question changed everything. Until then, we'd been busy tackling day-to-day issues, reacting to what was in front of us. But once he named the endgame and gave voice to what he really wanted, the tone of the meeting shifted, and we started setting goals for a future he had already envisioned on a grand scale.

Naming your endgame doesn't mean the answer is perfect or permanent. In fact, most of the time, it's not. What sounds right today may look different in six months or a year, and that's completely normal. That's where agility comes in.

CHAPTER TWO

Plans change. Priorities shift. Market conditions evolve. No one has a crystal ball, and you need to be prepared to roll with the punches. But just because the endgame might change doesn't mean you shouldn't name one. It's the act of defining the goal that creates alignment for everyone who works in the business. It's what helps teams focus their energy, set meaningful priorities, and start building toward something bigger.

VISION

I like to think of vision as the one-sentence statement hanging on the wall in the conference room that everyone in the dealership is familiar with.

The only problem is that sometimes, all the vision ends up being is a picture on the wall. You can probably see the problem with this; walk past the same picture enough times day in and day out, and you're going to end up completely ignoring it after a while. It becomes meaningless. For a vision to unite a business and become something everyone understands and is working toward, it needs to be reinforced daily. Vision only really takes root when it starts at the very top and defines the everyday operational culture of the business.

The dealer principal, or the ownership group in the case of larger organizations, has to be the one to initiate and shape the conversation by determining the vision. Whether they own a single location or fifty, they're the ones who set the tone for where the business is headed. They're the ones who have to answer, *What are we actually trying to build here?*

When that clarity is missing—when vision is left to the interpretation of individual managers—the business begins to fracture. Each operator starts crafting their own version of what success looks like. And while they may all be doing good work in their own right, the organization as a whole loses alignment. It stops moving forward together.

Without a strong vision that comes from the top, even the best strategies won't hold. No matter how well the business performs today, it will eventually start to lose cohesion.

MISSION

With the vision established by the dealer principal, the conversation shifts from vision to mission. Vision paints the picture. It's the image we place on the wall in our minds—that clear sense of what we're working toward. But once that picture is in place, we need to ask the next question: *How do we actually get there?*

That's where the mission comes in.

The mission describes the road we're going to walk, the actions we're going to take, and the behaviors we need to practice. When the vision is where we're headed, the mission is how we travel.

I often walk leaders through this by backing up just a little. If the vision is the future we're building toward—maybe it's *known for unmatched customer care*, or *a culture that retains top talent*—then the mission should describe the steps we commit to taking every day to make that future real.

It might be a short phrase or a few sentences. But whatever form it takes, it should describe the core of how the business intends to operate. Not just at the top, but across every part of the organization.

Sometimes, people expect mission statements to come out of the gate sounding bold and polished. But in practice, the best ones are often plainspoken. They reflect the work in front of you and speak to the values already at play. They make it easier to focus, not harder.

The mission also has to feel actionable. If it's just something nice to hear in a meeting or something you print on a brochure, it doesn't guide anything. But when it becomes part of how people talk, make decisions, and hold one another accountable, it starts to carry real weight.

In well-aligned teams, the mission shows up in the day-to-day. It's part of how new hires are welcomed, it's woven into how managers coach, and it shapes how departments prioritize, even when things get busy—*especially* when things get busy.

That's when you know a mission has taken root. Not when it sounds good, but when it makes choices clearer and helps people say, *This is the kind of organization we're building, and this is how we're going to do it.*

VALUES

When I help a team define its values, we don't start with aspirations; we take a look at what's already happening around the dealership. I'll ask the team to name people in the business who stand out, who everyone counts on, and who show up with consistency and heart. Then I ask, "What is it about them? What do they do that sets them apart?"

From those responses, we start to name the values that already exist. They're already part of the culture, just maybe not always consistently lived across the organization.

There's an exercise I like to use when working with dealership teams that's become a favorite called Mission to Mars.[1] It's one of the most helpful tools I've seen for getting teams to understand what their values really are.

The idea is simple: imagine Martians have landed on Earth and walked into your dealership. They don't speak our language. They can't read signs or mission statements. But they can observe.

What would they see?

They see how people treat each other. They watch how customers are greeted, how the shop is run, and how meetings are led.

---

[1] Adapted from *HBR, Building Your Company's Vision* by Jim Collins and Jerry I. Porras. Used by Gravitas Impact Premium Coaches.

CHAPTER TWO

If they're paying attention, they should be able to figure out the team's values just by watching what's actually happening.

In other words, values should be *visible*. They should show up in behavior.

In one organization I worked with, we'd spent years aligning everything to the company's long-standing vision and values. Then one day, an HR leader walked into a quarterly meeting and said, "We need a core values statement."

My heart sank.

We already had one! It had been there for years. But clearly, she'd never seen it, talked about it, or used it to guide her work. The problem wasn't that we didn't have core values, nor that they were unknown; they were written down plainly for everyone to see, and recited at all-hands meetings from time to time. The problem was that the cultural foundation had never been reinforced, shared, and truly *lived* by everyone, especially those in key leadership roles.

Once your values are defined, every time you gather as a team, you should be asking: "*How* are we living these values? *When* are we talking about them? *How* are we holding ourselves accountable to them? *How* and *when* do we celebrate them?" This way, they stay top of mind as part of the organization's culture.

PURPOSE

Too often, a dealership feels like a money machine. You walk in, and it's all about ads, inventory, and making a deal. It's not that the people running those stores are doing anything wrong. Most are doing what they were taught: sell the vehicle, hit the number, move on. But the culture is purely transactional, and when a business operates that way for too long, something gets lost.

To define your purpose, you should ask yourself: *why are we doing this?*

It's possible to build something more than a transaction-based environment. When I talk about building a dealership that truly lasts, I'm not just talking about margins or market share. I'm talking about becoming the center of the community, the kind of place people point to when they say, "That's where I go," and more importantly, "That's who I trust."

This doesn't happen by chance. It happens when the business is built on something I call Right Action.

Right Action[2] means something very specific. There are five key elements:

1. The right people
2. Doing the right things
3. In the right way
4. At the right time
5. For the right reasons

---

[2] This concept and method comes by way of David Herdlinger, founder of Kashbox™ Coaching, via the Trusted Advisors Network.

CHAPTER TWO

Right Action is how you shape customer experience and employee experience into something more than a checklist. It's how you move from transactions to relationships, and from short-term hustle to long-term loyalty. To this framework, I like to add a sixth element: *to achieve the right results*. I add this to continue to instill the "why" of what we're doing into the culture.

When you develop and retain the right people, they show up differently. They make decisions that serve the business and the customer, not just the sale. They know that integrity isn't a policy; it's the way they operate every day without being reminded.

Doing the right thing sometimes means saying, "You don't need that service today." It means helping customers stay in vehicles they can afford now, so they're in a better place when they come back a few years down the road. When you do that, you're not selling one car—you're earning the chance to sell three, plus potentially any boats, ATVs, motorcycles, or other vehicles they may want in the years to come. Maybe to the customer, maybe to their spouse or their teenager. That's how trust builds and how loyalty forms, and a customer for life is worth far more profit over time than just selling one service or vehicle tomorrow.

There's a small dealer group in my area that has never actually said out loud, "We do business by Right Action," but everything they do proves it. You can just feel it when you walk in the doors. Their customers won't go anywhere else. That kind of loyalty doesn't come from a catchy slogan or the best ad campaign; it comes from the *purpose*, the "why" of the dealership, that is woven into every moment and interaction.

I've had people tell me this approach is too idealistic and too soft for this industry. I disagree; I actually think it's the *only* thing that scales sustainably.

When you build a business around short-term wins, you're constantly chasing the next transaction. There's no margin for mistakes, and also no room for relationships. But when you commit to a purpose of Right Action, you plant seeds in your community that grow for years or decades to come. That's how you truly scale a business.

THE FORK IN THE ROAD

There's a moment every dealer has to face, whether they're leading a single rooftop or a large group of stores. It's a strategic fork in the road, and it usually starts with one simple question: are we here to close the next deal, or are we here to build something that lasts?

Both options can make money. That's part of the dilemma. You can push for today's transaction, squeeze as much as you can out of the deal in front of you, and move on. Or you can take the longer view—one that prioritizes relationships, builds trust, and leaves room for the customer to come back. Not just once, but over and over again. That's real Lifetime Customer Value.

That second approach is where real growth happens.

CHAPTER TWO

When you treat people like they're going to return, your decisions shift. You start coaching them through their options in a way that builds a genuine relationship. You're not just thinking about this first sale; you're thinking about the second sale, the third, and the vehicle their kid might need when they turn sixteen.

When you do it that way, something powerful happens. You're not just earning a sale; you're building a legacy. You're creating a base of customers who choose you on purpose and tell other people to do the same.

This is what Right Action looks like in practice.

Before I ever started working with automotive dealerships, there was one dealership in town, and *only* one, that my wife trusted. It was the only place she felt comfortable taking the car, and it wasn't about convenience or pricing. It was the way they treated her. It mattered to her that they made her feel welcome, like a guest. Not a transaction.

That might sound like a small thing, but for me, it's not. That feeling—comfort, trust, familiarity—is foundational. When someone says, "I love going there," it's not just about the technicians or the waiting room. It's because the people make you feel at ease. That's the difference between being treated like a person versus being processed like a customer.

If everything is treated like a transaction, then everything gets reduced to price. And when price is your only differentiator, you're not building a business—you're running a race to the bottom.

There's no room for growth in that model. You'll cap out eventually, because there's nothing left to offer except a discount. That's when people stop coming to you for what you bring to the table and start shopping around for whoever's cheapest that week.

But something entirely different happens when a dealership shifts its focus to building relationships instead of chasing transactions. I've seen it with my own eyes—teams that shift from just trying to hit the number to creating a place people genuinely want to come back to. That's when something real starts to happen. That's when the dealership stops being a stop on someone's to-do list and starts becoming part of the community.

I don't mean turning your showroom into an entertainment center or hosting food trucks periodically (unless that fits who you are, of course; I've known a few dealers who make fun and celebration a key element of their culture). You don't need to host an event to become known for treating people well, consistently and reliably, day in and day out.

People don't keep coming back to a dealership because of the brand on the building. They come back because of the relationship. It's the same reason you've got a favorite restaurant or a go-to plumber. You've got a person, not just a product. You want your dealership to become the kind of place where people say, "Having car trouble? I've got a guy. You've got to go see my guy." You become the person the customer can rely on for everything, not just transportation or recreational vehicles.

CHAPTER TWO

If you can do that, you've earned a place in people's lives beyond whatever deal you happened to be offering when they were in the market for a vehicle. You're no longer chasing short-term transactions. You're building something that can last.

That's how culture becomes the foundation. Vision, mission, values, and purpose aren't just pictures on the wall. They're tools to build a business people believe in.

KEY TAKEAWAYS ON STRATEGY

Here are five key takeaways from this chapter:

1. **True strategy begins with culture, not tactics.** A dealership must define its vision, mission, values, and purpose to guide decisions and actions at every level of the organization.

2. **Without a clear cultural foundation, dealership teams tend to operate in silos.** Employees rely on short-term fixes and drift away from alignment, which undermines both performance and trust.

3. **A strong vision provides long-term direction, while a mission offers a practical roadmap for daily behavior.** This ensures that every part of the organization is moving toward the same

goal with purpose and focus.

4. **Values are meant to be observed in action, not just written down.** They need to be reinforced through coaching, accountability, and consistent leadership behavior to truly shape the culture.

5. **The deeper purpose of a dealership—its why—must be relationship-building.** This leads to long-term loyalty, community trust, and sustainable growth.

DOWNLOAD THE ONE PAGE ROADMAP

Use this QR code to download a copy of the One Page Dealership Roadmap from thedealershipmanifesto.com.

CHAPTER THREE

ROADMAP STEP 3: RELATIONSHIPS

After finishing the strategy sessions with all Jim Kennis managers, my next step was to—appropriately, for the industry—take a road trip. It was time to visit each of the Jim Kennis stores in person and get a sense of how they operated when their managers were on their home turf.

My first few visits were uneventful; I saw exactly what I'd expected the managers' meeting, which was stores that ran at varying degrees of efficiency and effectiveness, all powered by localized, home-brew systems and processes that were wildly different store to store. Even with the inconsistency of SOPs, though, the stores were in pretty good shape, and it was easy to see why the Jim Kennis name had such a powerful draw in the region.

However, this changed when I visited one particular store. I had arrived in the morning and observed each department, all of which seemed to be doing okay; there were things to fix, as there were at every store, and the employees all had a distinctly stressed attitude, but for the most part, everything ran well. That is, until I observed the sales floor.

As I took a seat in the waiting area to watch how the sales team operated, I immediately noticed something strange. There was a couple standing near the showroom entrance—mid-50s, maybe early 60s. Clean-cut, well-dressed, the kind of people who didn't come in to browse. They were looking around and trying to catch someone's eye. The wife had her purse held with both hands, the way people do when they're not sure where to go. The husband kept glancing at the service desk, then back to her, clearly trying to figure out what the protocol was.

They didn't look upset, just a little lost, and uncomfortable in that way that happens when you walk into a space that seems like it should be welcoming but instead feels a bit like you've stepped into someone else's living room uninvited.

I waited to see what would happen, and to my dismay, waited another five minutes before anyone addressed the couple at all.

And when they *were* "addressed", it was at the bare minimum. The couple finally caught the attention of a young guy seated at the desk nearest to them in Sales. He looked over his shoulder and held up a finger. Not a rude gesture, just that universal "one second" sign. He turned back to his screen.

The couple stood there. Then moved a few feet over to the reception desk. But the receptionist was on the phone and didn't look up. Another salesperson walked by, phone in hand, nodded vaguely in their direction, and kept moving. A third was in a heat-

CHAPTER THREE

ed discussion with someone behind a glass office door.

The woman's face shifted first. She smiled again at someone who passed but then turned to her partner with a look that said, "I don't think we're getting any help here." I looked at my watch. They had been standing there for just over ten minutes.

They walked out.

No one stopped them. No one even seemed to notice they'd been there at all.

I let them get a few steps ahead of me, then followed them out the front doors and onto the lot. They climbed into a late-model Subaru, still in good shape but old enough that they were probably looking for something new. Maybe this was their first dealership stop of the day, or their last. Either way, I knew the chances of them circling back were slim.

I watched as they pulled out of the lot. Then I reached into my coat pocket, pulled out my phone, and called Greg.

He picked up on the second ring.

"Bill," he said. "What's up?"

"I'm at Sam's store on a visit," I told him. "As I was observing the sales floor, I watched a couple walk in. They were clearly here to buy. And I watched them stand there, unacknowledged, for ten solid minutes. Nobody made eye contact. Nobody stepped out from behind a desk. They left. I stood there and watched them go."

He didn't respond right away. I let the silence stretch.

"I don't think it's a one-time thing," I said finally. "And it's not just a sales process problem. It's a relationship problem. It's culture. Everyone on that floor looked stressed, distracted, like they were hanging on by a thread. Nobody had the bandwidth to look up and connect."

I could hear Greg exhale on the other end of the line.

"We've got to work with the managers," I said. "Not just on productivity and reporting. On relationships. Because we're not just losing customers—we're probably losing employees, too."

THE RELATIONSHIPS THAT MAKE YOUR BUSINESS

When I talk with leaders about what relationships they value most in the business, the first answer is almost always the same: the customers. That's who the business is all about, right?

Yes... but also, no.

You see, the relationship with the employees is just as important, and in many ways, *more* important.

Your employees may be the single biggest indicator of whether your dealership is going to succeed. If you're thinking about where to place your priorities—if you're trying to figure out what matters most when it comes to long-term growth—start there. Start with your people. That's not an opinion. It's a pattern I've seen play out in dealership after dealership.

When I get the question—where do people and talent fall in

CHAPTER THREE

the priority list for a dealership's success?—I always give the same answer. They're first. Always.

You can have a rock-solid strategy, offer a great product, and have solid execution, but none of that will last if your team doesn't hold together. If the turnover is constant, if the culture's sour, if you've got people more focused on protecting themselves than supporting one another, that strategy won't mean much. The product won't be enough to carry you. Execution will break down. You'll end up chasing short-term results instead of building something sustainable.

If you've got a revolving door of employees, it's going to show up everywhere; in customer experience, in your margins, and in the energy on your showroom floor. It will especially show up in the leadership pipeline you never quite get around to building.

If people aren't in place and thriving, the rest doesn't stick. The dealership doesn't grow. That's why your relationship with your employees is where everything, including your relationship with your customers, starts.

In this chapter, you're going to learn how to build a team of A-Players, how to make sure they stay, and how to continue to attract top talent into the future so that you have a deep bench waiting for when you need to bring on new roles. You'll also learn how the energy created by your employee relationships carries forward into the experience your customers have, and how to ensure your culture is the engine that creates raving fans who are loyal to your business for years to come.

WHERE CULTURE BEGINS: ATTRACTING A-PLAYERS

If someone asked me to build a blueprint for attracting top talent, I'd start with what you already learned in Chapter Two of this book: Vision, Mission, Values, and Purpose as the foundation of company culture.

I'd make sure the organization had done the work to clarify who they are. Once that's in place, you can invite others into something that feels solid and trustworthy.

Now, you're already in the great position of having your culture foundation nailed down, thanks to reading this book. So you're ready to get started on building the most attractive job ad possible.

When you're ready to hire, resist the pull to copy and paste the same generic job listing you've always used, the one that starts with a list of tasks and ends with a line about "competitive compensation" and "opportunity for growth." Anyone can write that. And the truth is, everyone *does*. That kind of language doesn't differentiate you. It also doesn't tell a potential employee anything about who you really are, how you work, or why they'd want to build a career with you instead of someone else.

Here's a condensed example of a hiring ad that has worked well for dealerships I've worked with (you'll need to edit to comply with

CHAPTER THREE

hiring laws in your state):

We're Not Hiring Just Any Sales Manager—We're Looking for *Our* Sales Manager

This isn't your typical job posting, because we're not looking for a typical candidate. Due to a well-earned retirement, we have a rare opportunity for a top-performing Sales Manager to step into a leadership role that's as much about culture, purpose, and values as it is about hitting numbers.

If you're someone who leads by example, lifts others up, and thrives in a collaborative, purpose-driven environment—read on.

But fair warning: we do things differently.

Here, you won't just meet with leadership. You'll be interviewed by the team who you'll be leading—the people who live and breathe the culture every day. They know what it takes to succeed here, and they'll know if you're the right fit.

What's in it for you?

- The chance to lead a team that actually wants to win together
- A culture where your voice matters
- Growth opportunities within a forward-thinking dealership
- Competitive compensation and benefits designed to reward top talent

If this sounds like the kind of place you've been looking for, send us your resume.

If it doesn't... well, you probably wouldn't like it here anyway.

That kind of message cuts through the noise. It signals that you're not just looking to fill a role—you're inviting someone into something intentional. You're setting the tone from the very first touchpoint that at your dealership, culture isn't just lip service. It's something people live out in meetings, in conversations, in how they treat each other when no one is watching.

When you say they'll be interviewed by the team, you're communicating trust and shared ownership. You're showing that your people have a say in who joins their team. That matters more than you might think. People don't just want a paycheck; they want to be on a team where they can do great work with people who inspire them to grow.

ONCE THEY'RE HIRED: MAKING SURE GREAT PEOPLE STAY

Hiring a great candidate is only the beginning. If you don't have the right environment ready for them when they arrive, you'll lose them just as quickly. Even if you manage to attract someone with impressive credentials, if there's no mentor in place to help them acclimate, or if the promises you made during the interview don't match what they experience on the floor, they'll start to feel it—and they'll leave.

The moment someone signs a job offer, do you have a plan to integrate them into your culture? Before the hiring decision is even made, do you actually know how to interview in a way that brings out more than surface-level responses? Too often, organizations post a job, ask a few generic questions, skip meaningful reference checks, and hope for the best. It's a missed opportunity at every level.

The consequences are huge. The cost of a bad hire doesn't stop at compensation. It damages morale, disrupts team dynamics, and slows down progress. It creates a ripple effect.

This is where I get a little fired up, because I've watched too many leaders fall into this trap. They don't set clear expectations during the hiring process. They sugarcoat the challenges. They skip over the hard truths. Then they're surprised when that promising new hire walks out the door a few months later.

When I'm in the room with a candidate, I say this plainly: "I want you to check us out as much as we're checking you out. I don't want you to accept this job unless you're confident it's right for you. Because if it's not, it'll disrupt your life—and I don't want that on my conscience."

We ask people to make a commitment to us. The least we can do is show them who we really are, and make sure we've created a place worth committing to.

EMPLOYEE RELATIONSHIP DOS AND DON'TS

1. THERE ARE NO HALF MEASURES ON CULTURE.

When I talk with people about their past jobs, especially during interviews, there's a pattern that shows up more often than anything else. It's not the pay. It's not the hours. It's not even the benefits.

It's the way they were treated.

Again and again, I hear the same stories. People were talked down to. They were yelled at in front of their teams. There was public shaming, passive-aggressive emails, or leaders who ruled with intimidation instead of integrity. These aren't occasional outliers. They're surprisingly common, and the damage they do runs deep.

One dealership I worked with had a situation boil over recently. I wasn't there when it happened, but the fallout was big. HR got pulled in. Legal threats started flying. It all stemmed from a complete breakdown in how people were speaking to each other.

When something like that surfaces, I try to ground the conversation in a more human way. I might say, "Who in your life do you hold in the highest regard?" Usually, the answer is someone

CHAPTER THREE

like a grandmother, a parent, or a mentor—someone who modeled respect and grace. And then I ask, "If that person were sitting right here next to you, would you speak the way you just did?"

Most people pause. They say no. The thought of using that tone or that language in front of someone they deeply admire changes the context completely. But every now and then, someone will shrug and say it wouldn't matter. That response always gives me pause. It's usually a sign we've got a mismatch in values—and potentially a bad fit for the role.

There's another version of this that shows up when someone brings in big numbers. Maybe they sell 20–25 cars a month and lead the board every quarter. They know their worth to the organization, and they use it as a shield. They say things like, "Who cares how I talk to people? I deliver." And that's where culture either stands or caves.

There's a saying in business: *culture is what you tolerate*. It shows up in what we let slide. And it gets defined not in the big moments, but in the quiet ones—when someone has the guts to say, "That's not how we treat people here."

I've seen leaders stay quiet in the face of that kind of behavior because they're afraid to lose the revenue. But I've also seen the opposite. I've seen someone draw a clear line, let that toxic top performer go, and create space for the rest of the team to breathe again.

What usually happens next is striking. The people who were

stuck working alongside that toxicity begin to rise. They step into the space that's been cleared. And without someone undermining the values of the place, they begin to contribute in ways leadership didn't even realize they were holding back.

2. PAY FAIRLY TO BUILD TRUST.

In the automotive world, it's not unusual for someone to walk into work one morning and find their pay plan has changed. Sometimes it's expected. Sometimes it feels like the rug gets pulled out from under them. And during COVID, I saw more of this than ever. The industry was upside down, and the money that poured in for cars, ATVs, boats, and motorcycles was—by many standards—unreal.

There were fewer cars, more demand, and a kind of bidding frenzy that no one could have predicted. In some places, salespeople barely had to sell. They just showed the car and let the offers roll in. And because many pay plans were tied to gross profits, those commissions soared. That's when a few dealerships stepped in and adjusted the pay plans downward. Not because of poor performance or cost-cutting, but because they felt people were making too much.

I don't agree with that approach. The groups I work with didn't do that. Not one of them adjusted pay plans downward during that time. And here's why: if you do that, you're sending a very clear

CHAPTER THREE

message. "When the business is booming, only the owners benefit. But when the market tightens, everyone needs to sacrifice." That kind of imbalance doesn't build a culture of trust.

Now, there are moments when changes to compensation are necessary—especially if something shifts on the manufacturer's end. If a customer satisfaction index (CSI) gets redefined or rebates change, then the math has to be revisited. But in most cases, when I hear people say their pay plan got cut, it's not because of metrics. It's because someone upstairs decided they were earning too much. Which really just means that someone didn't do a full audit on what the pay plan would look like and how it would impact the business's finances. Forecasting and validating pay plans for all conditions *must* be done upfront so there's no internal business need to change it down the road.

There's another way to approach it—one that treats compensation as a partnership. I was just advising a client who's hiring for a regional sales position. They were adjusting the comp structure, trying to stay competitive without overextending. My advice was simple: pay more for the right person. A true A-player will make you back that investment tenfold. And if you're not sure, structure the plan so it's performance-based with a six-month review built in. That way, you share the risk *and* the potential reward.

This reminds me of a personal story. A few years ago, one of my longest-running clients came to me and said, "I realized you're the lowest-paid person on my executive team—that's not right, and we need to change it." I'm not technically part of his internal team, but I've been with him for years. I thanked him for telling me, but I didn't want a handout. I asked him instead, "Do I bring economic value to your organization?" Without hesitation, he said yes. So I said, "Then pay me on the bottom line."

We agreed on a percentage, and planned to revisit it if it ever felt out of sync. Four years later, we've never had to change it. And during the COVID surge, we kept our commitments to each other. He never once came back to revise the deal. He's someone who in years past received his full annual bonus when he thought it would be cut—and he committed, then and there, he'd never let someone else feel the fear or uncertainty that he did.

There are plenty of dealerships where compensation changes happen behind closed doors, and people feel blindsided. But in the places that are run with integrity, compensation is part of a larger conversation—about value, about partnership, and about how we take care of the people who show up and give us their best. Those are the businesses that win in the long run.

3. DON'T WAIT UNTIL YOU NEED SOMEONE TO RECRUIT.

One of the biggest influences on how a dealership approaches hiring comes down to its size and stage of growth. A single-point store isn't going to operate the same way as a larger group with twelve or fifteen stores. Some groups are in rapid expansion mode, picking up new stores and growing leadership ranks. Others might be consolidating or even preparing for a sale. So there's no single answer to when a dealership should be recruiting—but there's one principle I come back to again and again.

The best-run stores don't wait until there's a gap to start looking. They keep their recruiting engine running all the time.

I advise dealerships to always have a careers page live on their site, no matter what. Not just for the positions that are open today, but for the roles they know will be important a year from now. Think of it like a college football program; they're not just filling this season's roster—they're always scouting for next year's starters. That mindset helps build a culture that looks ahead, rather than reacting when someone gives notice or a new store acquisition suddenly lands.

In organizations that operate this way, employees are usually informed about that steady drumbeat of recruiting. It's not a secret, and it shouldn't be threatening. I've worked with groups where leadership will say openly, "We're always looking for next year's leaders." That kind of transparency can actually strengthen trust—as long as the culture is healthy.

But here's the catch. This kind of ongoing recruiting effort only really works if the organization is known to be forward-thinking and growth-minded. If people don't see that as true, those job postings can create anxiety. "Are they trying to replace me?" "Is my job safe?" That kind of confusion only makes things worse.

In the strongest cultures, though, that ever-present recruiting presence is seen for what it is: *preparation*. It's the company saying, we're thinking about the future. We're planning ahead. And if we find someone who really fits our values, even if we don't have the perfect role open yet, we'll keep the door open or offer a different seat at the table until the right one opens up.

In my experience, the really good people are almost always working. They're usually employed, generally well taken care of, and more often than not, they like where they are. That's part of what makes them good—they bring a kind of steadiness that others notice.

But then something happens that's out of their hands. A decision is made at a higher level. A store closes. A company shifts direction. The rug moves beneath them, even if they've done everything right. They didn't cause the change, and they probably didn't see it coming. And now they're on the edge of something unfamiliar, trying to figure out what's next.

That's the moment I try to step into. Not as a recruiter with a pitch, but as someone who's genuinely interested in building a relationship. I don't need to know everything about their capabilities right away. What matters more is that we connect and that I reach out with respect, and without pressure.

What I've learned over the years is that if you want to build a team with real depth and integrity, you need people to understand

CHAPTER THREE

who you are before they're even thinking about making a move. They need to feel what it's like to be in a conversation with someone who sees them, not just their résumé. That trust, once it starts, creates a bridge.

Sometimes you have no choice but to be reactive. Someone leaves, and you've got to fill the seat. It's urgent, it's stressful, and it's far more common than we like to admit. Most of the time, that's how the hiring process works—out of need, not intention.

Once that scramble starts, it rarely wraps up in a week. It drags. Weeks go by. The pressure builds. Eventually, someone gets hired—often under duress—and that decision, made in haste, starts to ripple. It's a slow erosion. Culture doesn't collapse overnight. It gets chipped away, one misaligned hire at a time.

The wrong job for the wrong reason can disrupt everything. It can throw someone's personal life off course. It can set a team back six months. So we talk openly about it. We say: "We think we're good. But your version of good might be different. Let's both be sure."

DO YOU REALLY KNOW EACH OTHER?

Okay, you've attracted A-Players to your business, you've proactively set up a deep bench of future hires and brought on the right people in the present, and you have a great team starting to get to know one another. How do you fan the flame you've started to make sure it grows?

There are a lot of things you can do to build stronger relationships with your team. And no, I'm not talking about transactional gestures like handing out gift cards or tossing around employee-of-the-month awards. I'm talking about knowing the people you lead—really knowing them—and showing them that you're willing to show up, consistently, as a leader who sees them as more than a title.

You won't know everything about your team, and you shouldn't. But if someone's been with you for a while, it makes a difference to know what they're navigating in their personal life. It's a mistake to think those kinds of relationships are HR's job. That might sound harsh, but HR, by design, often functions in policies and procedures. What I'm talking about lives outside of policy. Your role as leader includes showing up in a way that feels human. That can only happen in a one-on-one relationship.

Years ago, I was working with a Volkswagen dealership that had a tough, tightly knit group of technicians. These guys had been together for years—decades in some cases—but when I first started meeting with them under the umbrella of leadership development, they sat in silence, arms crossed, letting me know in no uncertain terms that they weren't buying what I was selling.

Week after week, I kept showing up. Coffee. Donuts. Questions. Eventually, I shifted tactics. I stopped talking and started

CHAPTER THREE

listening. I ran a simple, low-stakes exercise: two truths and a lie. I wasn't sure how it would land. These weren't people who typically talked about themselves at work. They were practical, hands-on, task-focused.

But after some initial resistance, someone volunteered. Then another. And another.

It turns out, buried under uniforms and job titles were stories no one knew. One guy was a published poet. Another raised award-winning tulips. There was a baker whose confections were so good people placed orders months in advance. Another was a craftsman who had restored a classic car with his father-in-law. He actually invited me over to see it—a 1957 Chevrolet Bel Air convertible in red with a white top. I'd mentioned once that the '57 Bel Air was my dream car, and he lit up, telling me, "You're kidding, right? I have that exact car."

Then came the general aviation pilot. A room full of grease-streaked technicians, and among them was a man who spent weekends in the sky.

As the stories surfaced, I wrote each one on the whiteboard. This wasn't just a team of mechanics. This was a room full of artists, craftsmen, and adventurers. What struck me was how surprised they all were by each other; they'd worked side by side for years, but it seemed like they barely knew anything about each other.

"How is it that you've spent thousands of hours together, shoulder to shoulder, and you didn't know you were working next to a published poet? Or a guy who hand-restored a classic car? Or an award-winning baker?"

What happened in that moment—when they realized they didn't actually know each other—was the beginning of a cultural shift. A space opened up where people could be more than their job titles. They saw each other differently, and with that came a new level of respect.

CULTURE THE CUSTOMERS CAN FEEL

Now let's turn to the second most important relationship you have as a dealership leader: your customers.

Building one-on-one relationships with employees doesn't just create connection with your team; it sets the tone for how your team engages with customers. When employees have experienced authentic relationships inside the walls of the organization, they're more likely to extend the same care outward. I've seen it work. When employees have been part of something grounded in real relationship-building, they start to carry that forward in how they interact with the people who walk through the door. They remember not just a customer's vehicle but the story behind it—whose birthday it was, who the car was for, what moment it marked.

Those details are not transactional; they are relational. And they're often the reason customers come back.

CHAPTER THREE

When people roll their eyes at the word "culture," I know they're often thinking of vague slogans or motivational posters. But what we're talking about is something you can see and feel. It's the practiced, daily act of recognizing each other, caring about one another, and choosing to show up with the intention to serve. When leaders invest in that kind of culture, it changes how employees treat each other. And how they treat the customer.

You can tell when a team doesn't trust one another. You feel it the second you walk in. You see it in clipped tones and blank expressions. You see it in the way they rush through the transaction.

What you're witnessing is the absence of connection. When that's missing internally, it spills out into every customer interaction.

On the other hand, when employees are in an environment where they feel respected, supported, and valued, it shows. They learn to offer that same respect and care to the people who walk through the door. Not because there's a script telling them to do it, but because it's how the team operates. It's part of the air they breathe.

CUSTOMER EXPERIENCE: ROLL OUT THE RED CARPET

Imagine pulling into a dealership and feeling, from the very first moment, like you're somewhere that genuinely values you.

Not as a transaction or a number—as a guest.

You park your car in a space clearly marked for customers. No guessing, no wandering. As you walk toward the entrance, you're greeted by someone standing at the door. They're dressed professionally—not flashy, not stuffy—just right. They say, "Welcome. We're glad you're here today."

Your feet land on a red carpet. Not a skimpy three-foot runner that barely makes a statement; this one's wide, maybe six or seven feet across. It feels intentional. There's a path to follow, lined by velvet ropes that gently guide you forward, just like you'd see at a well-run event or venue that takes hospitality seriously.

You follow the carpet to the reception area. And the person there doesn't just glance up and ask what you need. They greet you like you've been expected.

"We're so glad you came in. Did you have a reservation, or are you just popping by today?" The tone is warm, not scripted.

And then—this is key—you're *not* told to sit and wait. You're not left to chase someone down or watch staff huddled in conversation, hoping to be noticed. The receptionist connects you directly to a sales consultant. Not just anyone, but someone who looks the part. Someone who respects the job enough to dress in a way that signals care and professionalism.

As you walk together, they offer you a refreshment. Maybe it's water or coffee. It's a small moment, but it says something. *We've prepared for you. You're worth our time.*

CHAPTER THREE

That's what service looks like when it's baked into the culture of a dealership.

I've lost count of how many dealership teams I've sat across from, but the question that always finds its way into the conversation is the same: how do we create a culture that actually values people—on both sides of the front counter?

My answer never changes. We start with the people who already work here. We start with the employees. Because if we don't build something meaningful with them first, we can't expect them to build anything meaningful with the people walking in the door. That disconnect is too big to bridge.

Sometimes I get pushback from store managers and dealership leaders. I might hear some version of, "You don't get it, this is a Ford store. We're not Rolls Royce."

As if the nameplate on the building should lower the bar for human decency. As if a customer choosing a Ford instead of a luxury badge somehow means they care less about being valued and respected.

I'll ask, "So Ford buyers don't want to feel welcomed? They don't want their time and their money treated with care?" That kind of thinking doesn't make sense—not in this business, not in any business.

Here's what I want when I walk into a dealership with my wife. I want someone to greet us at the door. I want to feel like my presence matters. I don't need anyone to roll out the theatrics. I need them to mean it when they say, "I'm glad you're here." Because odds are, I'm about to spend money I've saved or maybe don't even have yet. I'm making a big decision, one that might affect my life for the next five years. That kind of moment deserves someone's full attention and respect.

When we treat this like a one-time transaction, something important gets overlooked: you don't need to make all your profit from that one transaction. Over the life of a relationship—when they trust us, when they like how they're treated—they might come back for every oil change, every new car, and every friend they refer. That kind of loyalty builds a business. But it doesn't happen by accident.

It starts with mindset. The difference between "I have to help this person" and "I *get* to help this person" is one word—but it changes everything. That shift doesn't just change behavior. It changes the tone of the whole culture.

So what does that look like in real life?

1. Showing up ready.
2. Dressed like a professional.
3. Wearing a name tag so people know who they're speaking with.
4. Speaking clearly and respectfully.
5. Seeing people as guests, not customers.
6. Seeing each guest as an opportunity to help—not a number, burden, or line item.

CHAPTER THREE

Culture is not a theory. Culture is a habit. It shows up in how we greet each other, how we resolve a mistake, how we act when no one's watching. And it can't be reserved only for the people spending money with us. If our employees don't experience that care themselves, then asking them to deliver it to customers won't work. They'll spot the gap. And eventually, so will the customer.

The good news is, when we lead with care—when we focus on building something trustworthy, day by day—it creates a different kind of workplace, one that employees are proud of and that customers want to return to.

THE RELATIONSHIP ROI

There's a question I hear all the time from leaders:

When do we start to see the return? When is this going to yield results? When does this relationship turn into ROI?

The truth is, it already has.

The relationship itself is the return. When you lead from a place of service, when you invest in someone because you believe in them—not because you're waiting for payback—you've already begun to change the dynamic. You've created something of value. And while that might not immediately show up in a spreadsheet, it shows up in how people feel. It shows up in loyalty, in effort, in the way someone chooses to rise to the occasion because they know someone is standing beside them, not over them.

There's a real emotional lift that comes when we do something for someone else without attaching a condition to it. For me, that's one of the best indicators that we're on the path of Right Action. When we're building relationships, whether with team members or customers, and doing it from a place of sincerity, we're creating something that matters.

One of the clearest truths I've learned over the years is this: you can't create one kind of culture for your employees and expect them to turn around and offer something different to your customers. That kind of mismatch doesn't hold. People can feel it. They can see through it. And the ones doing the work? They won't buy into it.

When employees are treated with genuine respect, when they're seen and supported, they carry that into the conversations they have with customers. That's how culture lives and breathes. Not through posters or taglines, but in the tone of voice someone uses when answering a question. In the patience they show when something's gone wrong. In how they choose to help, even when no one's watching.

It's as simple as changing one word: "get" instead of "have."

You don't *have* to help that customer who just walked through the door. You *get* to. You get to make their day better. You get to solve their problem. And in the world of dealerships, that often means helping someone keep their life moving.

It sounds like a stretch at first, I know. But I had a conversation

CHAPTER THREE

once with a dealer who was trying to articulate the purpose of his store. We talked for a while, and he suddenly offered a pearl of wisdom I'd never heard before: "Maybe our purpose is simply helping people maintain their lifestyle."

He started breaking it down. What happens when someone's car breaks down? What happens when they're without transportation? Maybe they miss work. Maybe they can't pick up their kids, get groceries, get to the doctor. A lot of people build their lives around the freedom a car provides. So, when they walk into your dealership, they're not just there for an oil change or a new lease—they're there to get back to the life they've built. I was blown away by his definition, and I've carried it with me to other dealerships in the years since.

That's what I mean when I say "serve." You're helping someone return to the rhythm of their life. You're part of that. And when employees show up with that kind of mindset, customers feel it, and they remember it.

What could build more loyalty than that?

KEY TAKEAWAYS ON RELATIONSHIPS

Here are five key takeaways from this chapter:

1. **Employee relationships are foundational to dealership success.** When employees feel seen, supported, and valued, they become the foundation of everything else the business tries to build, including customer loyalty.

2. **Culture isn't a poster or a slogan; it's practiced daily in how people treat each other.** Whether it's how a new customer is greeted or how a technician is spoken to in the service bay, those moments shape the experience and define what kind of business you really are.

3. **Hiring must be intentional and proactive.** The best dealerships don't wait until someone leaves to start recruiting. They're always looking for potential team members who align with their values, and they take the time to build relationships before the role is even available.

4. **Compensation is part of culture.** When pay plans change suddenly or without transparency, it damages trust. But when pay is structured fairly and clearly, it reinforces a sense of partnership between the organization and its

CHAPTER THREE

people.

5. **Customer experience starts with employee experience.** A team that feels respected and taken care of will extend that same care to customers, creating the kind of environment where people feel welcomed, understood, and loyal—not just for one transaction, but for years to come.

CHAPTER FOUR

ROADMAP STEP 4: FINANCES

A few weeks after my individual store visits, I found myself headed back to one of the Jim Kennis stores in Boston. The store manager, Dan, had sent me a slightly panicked-sounding email a couple of days before.

Could I take you up on a one-on-one session? We're not making our numbers this month (or for the past few months) and I need to figure out a plan to fix it.

I arrived at the dealership before 8:00 am to observe traffic flow and customer interactions prior to our scheduled meeting at 10:00 am. Dan showed me into his office shortly before 10:00 and to a seat in front of his desk. "Thanks for coming," he said. "I appreciate you coming out."

"Of course. Tell me about what's been going on."

Dan launched into it immediately, and I let him talk for a while. "We just don't know what's going to happen this quarter," he said. "Leads are soft, traffic is unpredictable, and we've got interest rates scaring customers off."

"Okay," I said. "Let's pause for a second. You're telling me what you *don't* know. So let me ask you this: What *do* you know? What did your cash flow look like last month?"

Dan looked confused, then said, "Well, I know what our total sales were. I know we missed our target."

"Sure, but that's not what I asked. What's your *cash flow?*"

He was quiet.

It wasn't the first time I'd seen a manager or key leader at a dealership go quiet when I asked that question, and I knew that it had nothing to do with Dan not caring about the answer. In the work we'd done so far in group sessions, I knew him to be a good leader, a smart person, and committed to the work. But like a lot of operators I've seen in this business, he'd been conditioned to measure success by how many cars the store sold—and that wasn't the whole picture.

Cash? Forecasts? Burn rate? Those weren't numbers most managers like Dan usually kept in their daily line of sight.

"It's important to stop managing from the rearview mirror," I said. "Listen, the sales boom during the past few years wasn't real life. It was a windfall. It's over now, and things are going back to the way they were before, so you need to rely on the fundamentals to ride out the shift. That means knowing your cash flow down to the dollar week in and week out. You've got to know your costs, your forecasts, and your cash on hand. Not just monthly. *Weekly.* Daily, even."

CHAPTER FOUR

Dan looked like I'd just told him he needed to climb Everest. "I don't have any kind of forecast like that," he said. "How would I even start?"

If you're thinking Dan is an uncommon case in all the dealerships I've worked with, think again. A loose grasp of the dealership's financial picture is unfortunately common in this industry. I often compare it to driving on bald tires. You're not going to skid off the road as long as you don't hit any weather, debris, or particularly tight curves—but there's no road on earth where you won't run into one or all of those eventually.

In this chapter, you'll learn how to take control of the steering wheel and drive a clear financial picture down through every department in your business.

HOW'S YOUR CASH?

There's one truth about the dealership industry that's absolutely critical: *cash is the oxygen of the business.*

I didn't come up with that phrase, but it's one I learned years ago and have heard repeated by plenty of smart operators. And it's true. Without cash, *nothing* happens. It does not matter how good your team is, how strong your sales are, or how big your brand feels. Without cash flow, everything grinds to a halt.

We've all seen examples of it. Big organizations that look incredibly successful from the outside—growing fast, expanding locations, making headlines—suddenly find themselves out of business. Not because they lost customers overnight, but because they ran out of cash. They ran out of oxygen.

That's why, when we're talking about the financial aspects of a dealership, what we're really talking about is fiscal responsibility.

The first thing I notice in most organizations is that the dealer principal usually has a strong grasp of the big picture. They understand how the finances should work. But almost without fail, they're also looking for the best possible person to serve as their right hand when it comes to money. Whether it's an office manager, a controller, or a CFO, they want someone they can trust completely to manage the details.

When I say "watch the money," I'm not talking about guarding against theft or plugging leaks, although that's important too. The bigger challenge is broader and more strategic. It's making sure there's enough cash available to weather the inevitable storms that come in a cyclical industry.

The years 2020-2023 were *very* good for most dealers at levels that hadn't been seen in a long time, and probably won't be seen again for a while. Many dealerships made money hand over fist, almost in spite of themselves; if you had vehicles on the lot, you were going to sell them fast. But anyone who's been around a while knows that high profitability doesn't last forever. Our industry is inherently cyclical. Good years are always followed by tougher ones. That's just the nature of the business.

CHAPTER FOUR

Smart operators plan for the downturns not because they're pessimistic, but because they're realistic. They know the good years are the time to prepare for the harder ones.

That's why the best leaders use strong financial management to their advantage. They don't just enjoy the boom times; they use them to build reserves. They invest wisely. They make sure that when the market shifts—and it always does—they have the oxygen they need to keep breathing, keep moving, and keep leading.

A FINANCE CULTURE

You might be surprised how many employees at a business, even at the manager level, have no idea what's going on with the company's financials.

In fact, many key leaders at the top don't know. They've never been taught how to forecast cash from an operational perspective. So when I start to coach on finances, I go straight to cash flow and show them how to build a forecast they can actually use. Then we work on building day-to-day knowledge of the current cash flow and upcoming forecast into the culture, so that all managers, department heads, and employees are making decisions moment by moment based on that knowledge.

Over time, I've seen a pattern: the organizations that embrace this way of thinking early do far better than the ones that resist it.

One great example is a powersports dealership I work with. It's co-owned by two relatives, and their different backgrounds highlight why cash discipline matters so much. One owner is a CFO by training; the other came up through sales.

The sales-driven owner's mindset is, "Sell more stuff. Don't worry about the cash. It'll come." He's enthusiastic, high-energy, focused on the next deal. And honestly, that kind of drive is important. You need people who believe in growth and momentum.

But the CFO sees things differently. He's the one saying, "Stop spending until we get paid for what we've already sold." He watches the accounts receivable like a hawk. He knows cash doesn't just magically appear. He understands that without strong cash management, the wheels can come off the wagon, no matter how good sales look on paper.

Sometimes, their differences lead to lively debates—and that's a good thing. You need both perspectives to run a healthy business. The tension between driving sales and managing cash creates balance. It keeps the organization from swinging too far in either direction.

But it's not enough for just the owners or the CFO to understand this.

The real power comes when fiscal responsibility runs deep across the whole organization. It's not just about the people sitting in the finance office. It's about every manager, every department head, every person who has influence over how money is made or spent. Everyone needs to understand how cash really moves through the

CHAPTER FOUR

business. Everyone needs to see the connection between their actions and the company's ability to stay strong and grow.

FORECASTING MATTERS MORE THAN YOU THINK

You may or may not have been surprised to read that most leaders I work with can't answer up-to-date questions about their dealership's cash flow. Depending on which side you fell, you may also find this surprising: very few leaders, even the experienced, successful ones, even have a forecast.

Sure, they'll set targets for how many units they plan to sell, whether it's cars, boats, or something else. They'll map out rough expectations for each month, each quarter, or the year overall. They usually know those numbers off the top of their head.

But a real plan for how much cash will come in and how it'll be used? That's a whole different story.

Here's what usually happens. Someone will say, "All right, we need to sell 200 vehicles this month. If we sell 200 vehicles at $3,000 gross profit each, plus whatever bonus we get from the factory, we'll be in good shape." They'll add, "And the service department needs to do X." In just a few minutes, they have what they think is a forecast.

The problem is, that's not really a forecast. It's a loose estimation built on habit and hope rather than solid, thoughtful planning. It also tends to be reactive; for example, they'll sit there on August 20th talking about the September forecast, when in reality, they should've been talking about September at the beginning of the year.

They're working off what I call "profit and loss forecasting." They can tell you how many units they expect to sell. They can estimate the gross profit per unit. They have a general idea of expenses. But most of the time, they don't dig very deep into the real costs. They look at expenses *after* the fact, not before.

The best operators, the ones who really have their act together, take a different approach. They don't just forecast for units and gross. They forecast for cash. They forecast how much cash they expect to come in and how much needs to go out. They plan for it intentionally, not just assuming that if sales and service keep rolling, the cash will take care of itself.

That distinction makes a huge difference. Cash flow planning should be more than just survival; we're trying to do something bigger than just cover the bills month to month, right?

When you're only operating on the idea of, "Here's the kind of business we *usually* do," you're leaving yourself vulnerable. You're counting on patterns that can shift without warning. Without a month-to-month, intentional cash plan, you're relying too much on momentum and not enough on leadership.

Now, let me be clear: the leaders I'm talking about aren't careless or naive. These are smart, capable people. They have the experience

CHAPTER FOUR

and the intuition to run big businesses. But what I see, again and again, is that many don't take the time to go deeper—not because they can't, but because no one's challenged them to. Again, the mindset of "this is the way we do things" rears its ugly head and keeps people a little too comfortable.

But once you start planning cash with the same energy and precision you plan sales, you put your dealership in a position to thrive, not just when times are good, but when the inevitable storms come too.

Let me walk you through a real example.

One of my clients recently had a Saturday where they sold 120 new and used vehicles across their group of dealerships. That's a big Saturday; most weekends, they might move half that. And they expected to do it again the following Saturday.

On the surface, that looks like great news. Big sales numbers. Big momentum. But underneath, there's a different story—the story of cash flow.

You don't need a finance degree to understand it (I certainly don't have one!). I look at numbers from an operational, not an accounting, perspective. And operationally, here's what happens: when you sell 120 vehicles, you immediately set a series of financial obligations into motion.

Let's say the average finance contract on those vehicles is $40,000. Maybe half of those vehicles, around 60, involve trade-ins. Most of those trade-ins still have loans attached to them. That means the dealership has to pay off the lien holders to get clear titles.

So where does that payoff money come from?

It comes directly from the dealership's checking account.

If the average payoff on those trade-ins is, say, $10,000, that's $600,000 that needs to go out — immediately.

And that's just one piece of the puzzle. While the dealership is waiting for the finance companies to fund the new loans, they're sitting in a float. Millions of dollars moving, shifting, waiting. And that's assuming all the contracts are signed correctly and all the paperwork is flawless, which it often is not.

This is the real world of cash flow.

If a dealer and their leadership team don't actively forecast cash needs, they end up scrambling. They start shifting money from one account to another. You've heard the phrase "robbing Peter to pay Paul", right? It's one of the big sins in business, and you never want to do that.

You might get away with it for a while. But when the market softens—because it always does—or when borrowing power shrinks, the cracks start to show. Suddenly, strategic decisions like hiring, pay structures, and marketing investments are made in a panic because the cash just isn't there.

Profit might look good on paper, but if there's no cash to back it up, it's just a number. Cash is what keeps the lights on, keeps the paychecks flowing, and keeps the business breathing.

CHAPTER FOUR

MACRO VS MICRO

When it comes to cash management, there's a huge difference between taking a macro view and a micro view. And for a lot of dealerships, that difference is where the trouble starts.

A macro view of cash looks like this: you've got people handling accounts payable, accounts receivable, and all the basic financial operations. The dealer or key leader doesn't really dig into the details. They trust the systems in place, they assume the money is moving where it's supposed to, and life goes on.

A micro view, on the other hand, means the dealer or general manager is signing every payable check. That sounds like a massive job, and it is, especially for a large organization. But when leaders do it, even just for a season, something powerful happens. They start to really see where the cash is going.

I just saw this happen recently. A CFO told me the dealer had decided to personally review and sign the checks for a few weeks. It didn't take long for reality to hit. Suddenly the dealer was asking, "Why are we spending money on this?"

It's not that anyone was doing anything wrong. It's just that organizations, over time, tend to build layers of expenses that no one questions. Without a close, intentional review, costs creep up and cash starts leaking out.

The simple fix? You guessed it: a month-over-month cash flow forecast.

I'm affiliated with organizations that recommend going even further, forecasting cash flow for 36 months at a time. When I first tell people that, they look at me like I'm crazy. But the ones who take it seriously do incredibly well. It's not an easy habit to get into, but it's worth it.

So why don't more dealers do it? From what they tell me, it's because it feels like too much work.

Dealers and CFOs are already busy. Especially in bigger organizations, CFOs understand the value of forecasting. But they get frustrated when they take the time to build a detailed plan and then nobody uses it. They think, "Why should I spend all this time building something no one's going to look at?"

I worked for a while with a large group where the CFO had been there for over twenty years—a rare thing these days. Every year, he built a line-item forecast. Every revenue stream and every expense had a number assigned to it. It took months to get it right, going back and forth with the executive team to fine-tune the cadence. But once it was set, they actually used it. Every single week, they compared actual performance to the forecast.

They didn't wait until the end of the month, when it was too late to course-correct. They treated the business's finances like flying a plane constantly making small adjustments to stay on course.

That approach creates a culture where people aren't surprised by results. They aren't sitting around saying, "I thought our expenses

CHAPTER FOUR

would be lower," or "I thought our gross was higher." They *know* where they stand in real time, and they can act on it.

THE FINANCES ACTION PLAN

Running a financially responsible dealership isn't complicated, but it does require commitment. Everyone, not just the senior leaders, needs to know exactly where the cash stands, down to the dollar. In fact, knowing the cash position should be part of the dealership culture. It has to be a top priority, not just for the dealer or the CFO, but for the entire leadership team. Everyone needs to understand that being "pretty close" isn't good enough. Financial responsibility means knowing exactly where you stand, and it means treating that knowledge as a foundation for every decision.

To accomplish this, you're going to do the following three things:

1. Eliminate the mindset of "this is how we've always done it"
2. Create a cash flow forecast
3. Review the cash position weekly with all managers

Once the forecast is built, it has to be used. It has to become a living part of the leadership team's rhythm. Every week, leaders should be asking:

- How are we doing against our weekly and/or daily revenue forecast?
- How's our cash position compared to where we thought

we'd be?
- How many units and service hours have we sold?
- How much gross profit have we actually generated?

It's not about perfection—in fact, the numbers are almost always a little behind, just because of the fast pace of business. That's okay. The point isn't to have a flawless snapshot every second of the day. It's to have a living, breathing understanding of where you stand, so you can make smart decisions before problems show up.

In most dealerships, this kind of rigor just isn't the norm. And when you step back, it's not hard to see why. The dealership world deals with massive sums of money constantly moving—loan payoffs, finance contracts, and factory incentives and receivables all swirling around each other like clothes in a washing machine. It's easy to feel like it'll all "work itself out."

That's why it's critical to bring everyone into the financial conversation. Teach your managers what cash flow really looks like. Show them how their decisions impact the health of the business. Help them grow their understanding so they can grow their leadership. When you build a culture where everyone understands the financials, you're not just protecting your business; you're investing in its future. You're creating a team that can lead it forward, no matter what the market brings.

CHAPTER FOUR

THE WEEKLY CASH FLOW MEETING

In the weekly meeting where you review the financials and cash flow with all your key leaders, there are a couple of mindsets it's important to reinforce.

One: you're all entering a no-blame zone. That might sound a little soft for a conversation that's often about financial performance, but it's necessary. People want to point fingers when things don't go as planned. They want to blame another department or a person who didn't follow through. That instinct to assign fault is human, but it stops real progress from happening. So you'll want to start by stripping that away.

Two: ask them to think like investors. Instead of looking at each other as sales managers, service leaders, or department heads, ask them to step into a different frame. Tell them to imagine they're a board of directors or a group of investors. Now you're not talking about daily tasks or missed quotas. You're asking a different kind of question: If you were investing in this business with your own money, what kind of return would you want to see? And what would it take to actually get it?

What you're really building is financial acumen as part of your company culture. You're teaching people to recognize how the rise and fall of cash shapes what they can and can't do. You're showing them how their work connects to outcomes they may never have seen as their responsibility. Once they can see that, they can work backwards to figure out exactly what they and the people working under them need to do to make the company's mission happen.

GET EVERYONE THINKING LIKE AN OWNER

In one dealership I worked with, we started holding a daily meeting with six key managers. It wasn't anything fancy. Just a 10- to 15-minute huddle where the controller reported one thing: the previous day's bank deposits. Not the balance, not the forecast, just deposits.

At first, it felt mechanical. Numbers were read off. People nodded. But after a few days, the questions started. "Why were deposits down yesterday?" "What happened to Friday's deals?" "Is there a reason we didn't see more from service?"

That's when the learning kicked in. One day, someone asked why deposits were unusually low. The answer? Contracts that hadn't been funded yet. They were sitting three days late, waiting on something small—maybe a signature, maybe a missing form. But those contracts represented a million dollars that hadn't hit the bank. Suddenly, that daily meeting wasn't just about looking at the numbers; it was about understanding what was behind them.

Most dealerships are flooded with data. They've got KPIs, dashboards, and daily reports. But the data doesn't mean much unless people know what it represents *and* feel responsible for it. And they won't feel responsible for it unless they're part of the conversation.

We didn't need every manager to know the exact cash balance at every moment. The flow of cash in a dealership is too dynamic for that. A store can end Friday flush and find itself upside down by Monday morning because of trades that were paid off over the weekend. What we needed was awareness. We needed curiosity. We needed to replace "they've got it covered upstairs" with "I understand how my role affects the bigger picture."

When managers start thinking that way, they begin to think beyond their function—sales, service, parts—and instead think like operators. The goal isn't to turn every manager into a CFO. It's to help them see how their decisions impact the business. When they understand that, they become better partners in driving the outcomes that matter.

Curiosity is powerful, but it has to be supported by transparency. I've seen dealerships give managers limited financial access—just the KPIs they're "responsible" for. Sometimes that works. But when managers don't understand what the line items mean, it limits their ability to lead. Worse, it can create a sense of detachment that will spread throughout the company culture. The last thing you want is for every employee to consider finances "someone else's job".

Finance managers also impact cash flow significantly. The gross profit on a vehicle sale, in most situations, comes from the finance office in the form of points/margin on the loan, and warranties, extended contracts, maintenance agreements, tire and wheel protection, fabric and paint protection, aftermarket customizations, etc. This is even more true for marine operators and powersports dealers. Every single boat or vehicle that is sold is highly customized and personalized to the buyer; nearly every nut and bolt is unique. A lot of the margin is coming from that customization. This impacts cash flow because they have the ability to generate a lot more profit on the products than the actual sale of the vehicle. Also, depending on the down payment, the cash flow will be impacted; a smaller down payment means a bigger hit to cash flow.

In a lot of dealerships, though, considering finances "someone else's job" is unfortunately the habit. The operational managers—sales, service, parts—tend to focus on their lanes. They're good at what they do. They know how to sell a car, manage a team, and keep the service drive running. But ask them where the money goes, how it moves through the business, what's impacting cash flow this week, and most will point upstairs. "That's for the dealer or the CFO to worry about. My job is to sell."

It's understandable; these roles are demanding. They come with their own set of daily fires to put out. But when you keep financial fluency siloed at the top, you limit what the business can become.

On one side, managers want to trust that leadership is watching the financials. On the other, they're being held accountable for performance. That gap can create a kind of fog. You're expected to drive results, but you don't see the whole picture. It's hard to make

CHAPTER FOUR

smart decisions when the numbers feel like a mystery.

The truth is, you can't build a strong culture—or a sustainable business—without operational leaders who understand how every dollar works.

That's why I encourage the mindset shift and financial practices you've learned about in this chapter at every dealership I work with.

I want every operational manager thinking like an owner.

That doesn't mean they need to see the full general ledger or become accountants overnight. But they need to be aware, ask questions, and truly understand the cost of what they're doing and what happens when cash gets tight.

Everyone in your dealership should understand the money.

Because when everyone understands the money, everyone protects it.

KEY TAKEAWAYS ON FINANCES

Here are five key takeaways from this chapter:

1. **Cash is the oxygen of the business.** Without a disciplined understanding of cash flow—weekly, daily, and even transaction by transaction—dealerships put their operations at risk, regardless of how strong their sales numbers may look on paper.

2. **Building a finance culture starts from the top down.** It means teaching every leader, not just the dealer principal or CFO, to think in terms of cash movement, understand how decisions impact the bottom line, and forecast intentionally rather than relying on historical patterns.

3. **Forecasting isn't just about projecting unit sales or gross profit.** It's about creating an accurate, actionable plan for how money will move through the business, and using it to guide decisions before problems arise.

4. **The most effective dealerships build financial awareness into their leadership rhythms.** They hold regular meetings to review cash flow, remove blame, and challenge leaders to think

CHAPTER FOUR

like investors who are responsible for long-term returns, not just short-term wins.

5. **Managers need to think like owners.** When they ask questions, understand how their departments affect the bigger picture, and see themselves as part of the financial health of the company, they shift from simply managing to truly leading.

CHAPTER FIVE

ROADMAP STEP 5: SYSTEMS

After getting things in shape with Dan at his store, I was immediately back in a tough situation at a Jim Kennis store. This time, though, the store manager wasn't as happy to see me as Dan had been.

Kyle, the manager of another store, had already thrown up some red flags for me at the all-manager sessions. He was always quiet, arms crossed, wearing that half-checked-out look that tells you someone's already made up their mind. He never said anything directly, but his posture said enough: *I don't need this.*

I'd gotten a lot out of the other store visits—frank conversations, real questions, and a few nervous laughs when I brought up things people had been avoiding. But when I arrived at Kyle's store, I could immediately tell this visit would be different.

Kyle didn't just seem closed off. He seemed like he wanted me gone before I'd even stepped inside.

When I arrived, Kyle walked me through the showroom politely enough, but without any eye contact for more than a second or two. We made our way to his office. He closed the door, and before I could sit down, he said, "I'll be honest with you. I don't really see the point of this."

I smiled, trying to keep things light. "You mean of me being here, or the work I'm doing with the group?"

He shrugged. "Both, I guess. I've run this store for five years. We're profitable. My team knows what they're doing. I don't need someone coming in to tell me how to fix what isn't broken."

I sat down and looked at him carefully. "I appreciate that, Kyle. And I don't doubt that you've worked hard to keep this place running. But Greg asked me to visit every store, and I'm here with no assumptions—just questions. Would you be open to walking through some of your systems with me?"

He leaned back in his chair. "I mean, we don't have processes written out. We've got a rhythm here. People know their roles."

"That's helpful to know," I said. "Could I see how you handle something specific—like how you onboard a new hire, or how you handle a customer complaint?"

Kyle gave a quick shake of his head. "We don't really have a checklist or anything. It depends on the situation. That kind of stuff's hard to standardize."

That's when it clicked. It wasn't that his systems weren't documented. There *were* no systems. There wasn't structure. There was Kyle—and everything revolved around what he personally managed. Which meant if he stepped away, things would fall apart.

CHAPTER FIVE

"A strong store runs on more than one person's muscle memory," I said. "Systems give people something to rely on, even when you're not in the room."

Kyle crossed his arms again. "I don't need systems to get results. The numbers are solid."

"That might be true today," I said, "but I've walked into stores where the numbers looked solid until one person left, or a market shift hit, or a key team member burned out. And everything changed."

I might as well have been trying to convince the soda can from his lunch sitting on his desk. He didn't say anything, just stared out the window.

When I called Greg later that afternoon, I cut straight to the issue.

"We need to talk about the South Boston store," I said. "I don't think Kyle's the right guy for that store. He's holding it together with sheer force of habit, but there are no systems. No SOPs. He won't take input, and he doesn't think he needs to. As long as he's in that role, nothing's going to change."

Greg didn't sound surprised. "Thanks for being straight with me."

"He's not a bad guy," I added. "But he's closed off. And you can't grow an aligned organization with people who won't even consider a different way forward."

Kyle embodied an issue I see in dealerships all the time: a lack of standardized systems, and managers and leaders who dig in their heels about the need for them.

In this chapter, you're going to learn why it's so critical to the growth of your dealership to have solid, documented, and well-understood systems in place—and you'll learn how to make important changes to systems when you run up against resistance.

THE NUTS AND BOLTS OF SYSTEMS

Before we get into what's going wrong with systems in dealerships, we have to zoom out for a moment. Because the truth is, like Kyle's store, a lot of dealerships don't have systems in place to begin with.

When I say "systems," I'm not talking about something theoretical or out of reach. I'm talking about the day-to-day, nuts-and-bolts ways that things get done. How a sale gets closed. How a vehicle gets delivered. How service tickets get processed. Systems are the behind-the-scenes scaffolding that hold the entire operation together.

At many dealerships I work with, processes aren't just inconsistent, they're totally undocumented. Standard Operating Procedures (SOPs) either don't exist, or if they do, no one knows where to find them or if they're still current. What ends up happening is that each person in each department shows up with what worked at their last job and tries to apply it.

CHAPTER FIVE

At first glance, this can seem like resourcefulness. People are trying to make things work. They're leaning on what they know. But eventually, it creates a Frankenstein effect: a patchwork of different systems cobbled together that don't speak to one another, don't scale, and don't lead to consistent outcomes.

So now you've got one person in Sales doing it their own way, another person in Service with a completely different approach, and someone in Finance who shrugs and says, "I've kind of got my own way of doing it."

That phrase again! If you only take one thing away from this book, it's to stamp out that way of thinking whenever you come across it.

When someone says that to me, I like to gently confront them: "Well, let me ask you, how's that working for you?"

Because what I tend to find is that these personalized, undocumented systems work… until they *don't*. Then, when something goes sideways, nobody can figure out why.

Missing systems are visible all over your dealerships wherever you see stuck points. Bottlenecks. Workarounds built on top of workarounds. Without standard, documented systems, each department ends up reinventing the wheel.

That's the moment when the team begins to lose faith in the organization's ability to support them. That's the cost of not having documented, tested, and agreed-upon systems. It's not just inefficiency; it's demoralizing to the entire team.

THE SOLUTION: SLOW DOWN TO BUILD WHAT WORKS

Before you go barreling ahead into creating all new systems, reflect on what you already have.

First, you need to confirm that a problem you're having *is* a systems problem. This step is essential. It's easy to jump to conclusions or blame individuals when things break down. But most of the time, it's not a people problem—it's a process problem. When you've got good people trying to do their best and they're still struggling, it usually means the system is failing them, not the other way around.

Sometimes, though, the problem really might be with a certain individual who's in the wrong role, or not aligned with the company's values. Make sure that's not the case before you start messing around with your systems, because—and we'll go into more detail on this later in the chapter—changes in process are inherently destabilizing and need to be carefully handled.

Once you're clear on that, the next step is getting agreement that everyone needs to follow a proven system or process. This isn't about control or micromanagement; it's about clarity, consistency, and collective support. When a team operates from a shared system, they know what to expect from each other. They can troubleshoot more easily. They can train new hires more effectively. They

CHAPTER FIVE

can scale.

Then comes the work of breaking down the current system, step by step. Take a good, honest look at what's actually happening. Not what you think should be happening, or what's written in a dusty manual from five years ago, but what people are doing *right now*. This is where you look for the bright spots: the parts of the process that are working really well. Just as important, you'll also diagnose what's *not* working.

This part of the process is critical, because too often, we throw out the baby with the bathwater. We get so frustrated with the whole system that we scrap it completely and start over. That might feel productive in the moment, but it can actually set you back; even in a messy Frankenstein system, there are usually some pieces that work beautifully. You want to keep those.

Once you've identified the stuck points—the bottlenecks, the duplications, the miscommunications—you can zero in on them and start asking questions with an eye toward how a change will ripple through the rest of the dealership. Avoid making changes in silos. Your job is to design something cohesive that connects across departments and roles.

Building strong systems takes time, patience, humility, and a willingness to listen. If you put in the effort, the payoff is enormous. When a dealership operates with clear, consistent systems, everything changes. People stop stepping on each other's toes; leaders stop firefighting; teams start trusting each other and the process.

Most importantly, customers feel the difference.

I recently spoke to a friend who had two very different experiences within the same dealership. On the customer service side, the process was impeccable. "We walked in and were immediately in the flow," she said. "It was like they were reading our minds. Anything we needed, they anticipated. Every question we had, they had a great answer for. Picking out the right car for us was a fast, efficient process."

Unfortunately, the sales handoff to finance was where the wheels came off. "Suddenly it was like we were dealing with two different companies who share a building but never talk to each other," she continued. "Everyone was polite, but the amount of information we had to repeat or correct completely ground the process to a halt. We'd describe things Sales had told us, and Finance would say, 'I'm not sure why they told you that.' We had to totally rework the plan we had come up with in the sales process, and in the end we weren't even sure we wanted the car anymore. We decided to leave and think about it."

You can probably guess what happened next: she ended up going to a different dealership where the process was smooth and cohesive, and walked out with the car she wanted in under two hours.

If your dealership is feeling chaotic, inconsistent, or stuck, don't just power through. Your relationships with your customers *and* your employees rely on systems and processes that leave frus-

CHAPTER FIVE

tration in the rearview.

THE IMPORTANCE OF DOCUMENTATION

"Do you have documented systems in place to run the organization?"

When I ask this question, I typically get a quick affirmative. "Sure. Yeah. Of course."

My natural next step is to ask, "Great—can you show them to me?"

That's when the pause happens.

More often than not, the documentation either doesn't surface, or it turns out to be outdated and no longer relevant. Nobody is lying, but what people typically mean is more like, "We have some things written down somewhere."

But when it really comes down to it—when someone new joins the team and needs to be trained, or when a process starts to break down—those documents are either missing altogether or don't reflect the way things actually work today.

Most dealerships don't have clear documentation that a new person could look at and follow step-by-step. Without documentation, there's nothing to refer to, no foundation to rely on, and no consistency across people or departments.

If a process isn't written down, how is anyone supposed to follow it?

Without documented processes, even simple tasks around the dealership become a game of telephone. The message gets passed from one person to the next, and somewhere along the way, it shifts. A detail is lost. An assumption is made. A shortcut gets introduced. And eventually, the original process—the one someone worked hard to design—becomes unrecognizable.

What typically happens then is something that looks like resourcefulness but is actually the road to chaos: when people can't find documentation for how something is supposed to work, they make their own. That might seem like a solution in the moment, but it creates a new set of problems. The process they create might not match the existing one, or it might conflict with what another team is doing altogether. Now, instead of one missing system, the organization has multiple, disconnected versions.

Even simple tasks can spiral into confusion. Take something as basic as accepting a payment when the cashier isn't available. Without a written policy to follow, people start coming up with their own solutions. Sometimes those solutions lead to serious risks.

The key takeaway here is that when everyone is improvising, even with the best intentions, things start to go sideways.

CHAPTER FIVE

TOOL: THE DEALERSHIP HEALTH ASSESSMENT

So, how do you fix the issue? Where do you start?

Before you create a thick training manual with an SOP for each and every dealership system, you'll need to identify exactly where the systems gaps are. And to do that, you'll need to get insight from everyone who works in your organization.

When I work with dealerships struggling with their systems, the first thing I ask them to do is complete a simple diagnostic called the Dealership Health Assessment. The assessment gives you your team's interpretation of how things are going across eight core functional areas of the business. It's incredibly revealing.

TAKE THE DEALERSHIP HEALTH ASSESSMENT

Use this QR code to take the full Dealership Health Assessment.

In fact, I've had leaders say they're stunned by what comes back. You know the feeling you get when you bring your car in for a multi-point inspection and the service tech tells you it failed twenty out of twenty-seven checks? "The car seemed fine!" But now you're looking at the data, and you can't unsee it. The car is *not* fine.

That's what this tool does for an organization. It reveals problems you didn't even know you had—and that would have turned into rot if left unidentified.

THE ASSESSMENT'S IMPACT

What the assessment shows is how aligned or misaligned the team really is. One of the statements on the assessment, for example, might be: "Our organization always hits its strategic objectives." Respondents rate that on a scale from one to five. Five means "absolutely, all the time"; one means "never".

More often than not, people working in the same building, in the same meetings, on the same projects, will rate that question in completely opposite ways. One person checks a five. Another checks a one. When you review the assessment, your first response is usually disbelief: "How is that possible?"

It's a fair question. These are people who've been spending fifty, sixty, even eighty hours a week under the same roof for years. How could one person believe the team *always* hits its goals, while someone else doesn't even recognize the conversation?

CHAPTER FIVE

It happens all the time. And when it does, you don't just have a performance issue—you have a communication gap, a clarity problem, and a culture question all rolled into one. Multiply that across seventy or eighty items on the assessment, and patterns start to form. The Dealership Health Assessment helps you name them.

AN UNBIASED VIEW

Here's why this tool matters so much: it takes your personal opinion out of the picture.

The dealer principal or general manager isn't just calling a meeting and telling people what they *think* is wrong. They're able to hold up the assessment results and say, "Here's what you said about your own organization."

This part can be uncomfortable. Sometimes leaders push back on what they see. Sometimes they try to explain it away. I've had dealers flat-out reject the results of these assessments. One in particular called a meeting and brought everyone together—about twenty-five people, including the entire service department. He stood up in front of the room and said, "I just reviewed the results of the survey, and I don't believe any of it." Then he announced, "We're going to do it again."

What do you know? When they took the assessment the second time, the results were glowing.

Of course they were! That's what happens when people feel like they're being tested, not heard.

When the person at the top sticks their head in the sand and dismisses the data, it doesn't correct the problem—it just drives it underground. After all, the *appearance* of improvement isn't the same thing as progress. And when a team feels like they have to manage how they answer instead of being honest, the real issues get harder to see, not easier.

WHEN EGO GETS IN THE WAY

If you've been managing or leading a dealership for long, this probably won't surprise you to hear: most people *really* don't like having to learn a new system.

One of the things we've recently implemented in a larger dealership group I work with is a requirement that anytime a new salesperson is hired, their start date has to line up with our next scheduled sales training. It's a shift from what used to happen, where people would be hired and then sit around for a couple of weeks without much structure. Now, when someone's brought on, I get contacted, and I take them through a two-day sales training.

We follow a very specific agenda in that training. It's not just about skills; it's about helping people understand the systems that drive how we operate. That part is key. But I've noticed we get the most pushback from people who already have experience. By the second day, I usually start hearing the same thing: "I kind of do it

CHAPTER FIVE

this way," or "I've got my own way of doing it."

That's when I know it's time to pause and step back. I'll say, "I hear you. I understand how you used to do it." And I mean that; I'm not trying to erase their experience.

But I follow that with, "Here's how we do it here. And here's why that matters."

It matters because we're not training people just for the store they start in; we're creating opportunities for growth. Someone might begin at a smaller location and later move into a larger one. If they don't understand the systems we use across the group, they're going to run into friction when they try to integrate with a new team. Well-documented systems and processes allow people to grow, evolve, and move through the organization without losing momentum.

A lot of the time, what gets in the way is ego. I say that with compassion; we all have it! When someone has done something one way for years and it worked, it can be hard to open up to a different method.

That's where I try to encourage people to shift from defending what they know to simply being curious. I'll say, "Try it. Test it. Measure it before you say no."

I'm not asking anyone to abandon what they've learned. I'm asking them to give the process a real try. Once they do, they usually see the value for themselves.

EFFECTIVE CHANGE MANAGEMENT

Change management today, especially in dealership environments, often follows a familiar pattern.

It starts at the top. A general manager decides on a change and announces it: "This is what we're doing now."

And… that's it. That's usually as far as the rollout goes. The expectation is compliance, not discussion.

Can you really blame employees for being resistant to that kind of change?

The way it needs to happen starts in a completely different place. Once the Dealership Health Assessment wraps up, the first step for leadership is to slow down and look closely at what the assessment surfaced. Gaps in systems and processes aren't just numbers on a page; they point to real stories unfolding across departments.

CHANGE MANAGEMENT PHASE ONE: DIAGNOSE THE PROBLEMS

Gather your department leaders for a working session to review findings with curiosity instead of judgment. Start by breaking down the data by department; ask leaders and frontline staff where things felt misaligned or unclear. Invite team members who interact with the process daily to share what gets in the way of doing their best work. Look for patterns—where are the bottlenecks, the handoffs that falter, the processes nobody seems to own?

Here's the step-by-step:
1. Review assessment data with all department leaders.
2. When a systems issue is identified, invite feedback from frontline team members directly involved in the process.
3. Pinpoint areas where communication breaks down or where delays happen; these are your most likely areas of improvement.
4. Identify where processes lack ownership or clear accountability; this is where structure is missing in your systems.

CHANGE MANAGEMENT PHASE TWO: CREATE YOUR ACTION PLAN

After identifying the gaps, the next step is to ground those insights in action. Remember, you're not going to be able to fix everything at once! Start with what matters most.

Here's the step-by-step:
1. Prioritize the areas that impact people and performance, then schedule time to co-create solutions.
2. Write new processes down. Make them visible, testable, and revisable.
3. Talk these new processes through with the people they'll affect, especially frontline staff. They do the work day in and day out, and they'll catch things you might miss.

4. Build in moments for reflection as the new systems roll out, so everyone has a chance to share what's working and what isn't.

QUESTION YOUR ASSUMPTIONS

A word of advice: your first instinct on what needs to change in your dealership may not be correct. In fact, it's often *incorrect*. This is where the Dealership Health Assessment is so important; it's the ultimate test of your assumptions.

For example, recently I worked with a large dealership group that had originally reached out wanting formal management training for their team. But in our first meeting, when I asked them why, they looked at me confused.

"It's something many of our managers are missing. It'll raise the bar for all of them and help fill in some gaps," they explained.

"Great," I replied. "Can you get specific? What is it you're seeing or not seeing that led you here? If the issue is that your managers lack the right skills, what would be different if they had them?"

I wasn't trying to be difficult. I just wanted them to pause and think it through. My gut feeling was correct; they couldn't answer my questions in any kind of substantive way. They were prepared to drop a ton of cash on training for dozens of managers, and no one had asked *why*.

Formal management training might have made them feel like

CHAPTER FIVE

they were doing something to improve the business, but there was no way of knowing if it would actually get results, because this group had never openly identified and diagnosed their issues. If everyone feels good while the business continues to burn cash, then the feel-good moment doesn't mean much.

They needed to do a Dealership Health Assessment before any assumptions could be drawn or actions determined. Luckily, they agreed to this without any pushback. When the assessment came back, and the results were unpacked with the whole leadership team, it was abundantly clear that management training was the *last* thing they should be spending money on at that point in time. They had a ton of work to do to clean up not just their systems, but also their culture, before investing in that kind of fine-tuning.

DON'T DUMB DOWN, EDUCATE UP

The Dealership Health Assessment works because it's hard to hide when you put a mirror up to the business.

But nothing in the assessment matters unless you take *action*. You might be surprised how easy it is to identify and diagnose your problems, then stop without assigning specific responsibility to making the changes.

Why is this? My theory: analysis is more comfortable than change. To get your dealership systems in order, you're going to need to get uncomfortable—and you're going to need to bring your employees along for the ride.

Once, after I came off stage from speaking at an industry event, a dealer came up to me and said, "Everything you described on stage—every single part of it—is exactly what's happening in my store."

I told him, "Sorry to hear that. What are you going to do about it?"

That's the turning point. Some people get to that moment and take action. Others get to that same moment and decide not to move forward. I've had plenty of people complete the assessment, see the results, and then choose not to do anything about it.

That's always their choice. No one has to fix what they're not ready to face. I give them the truth as kindly as possible: "You don't have to do this work. But if you want the organization to get better, these are some of the things that will need your attention."

Improvement isn't automatic. It takes intention, clarity, and the willingness to take responsibility for the things that are broken. That *only* starts when the person at the top says, "I'm ready."

At the dealership, everyone is working hard, and it's a tough sell to ask them to put even more on their plates. But that's how people get siloed in their experience and perspective. Without cross-functional systems and the commitment to accountability, pretty soon you have an organization where each person knows how to do their part, but there's very little shared understanding of how the business functions as a whole.

CHAPTER FIVE

That's the mindset you need to shift. To really make change, employees need to go from thinking, "How do I do my role?" to, "How do we elevate the entire organization?"

What you're working toward is building fluency across the leadership team, not just in operations, but in the full business of the dealership. When leaders understand the bigger picture, they're able to make stronger decisions in real time. They stop reacting and start thinking more strategically. That shift doesn't just improve performance—it raises the level of leadership throughout the dealership.

Systems are complicated. Building great systems is high-skill work. You need to trust your team to do that work, and empower them with the knowledge and transparency to make your business take off. There's no need to dumb down what people are capable of understanding; it's time to educate up.

Because when leaders know how the business actually works, they lead differently. That's where change really starts to stick.

KEY TAKEAWAYS ON SYSTEMS

Here are five key takeaways from this chapter:

1. **Documented systems are non-negotiable.** Many dealerships run on individual habits and muscle memory, which leads to confusion, inconsistency, and operational breakdowns when one key person leaves or the market shifts.

2. **Diagnose before you design.** Effective systems begin with an honest assessment of what's really happening, including input from frontline staff, so the solutions you create are rooted in reality and built to last.

3. **Write it down, or it doesn't exist.** Without clear documentation, even simple tasks become inconsistent and risky, while accessible SOPs give teams the structure they need to train, scale, and serve customers well.

4. **Use data to drive alignment.** The Dealership Health Assessment reveals hidden breakdowns, misalignment, and blind spots, creating a clear and objective foundation for system improvements.

5. **Change requires humility and shared responsibility.** Real transformation happens

CHAPTER FIVE

when leaders drop their egos, involve their teams, and shift from siloed thinking to educating people across departments on how the whole business works.

CHAPTER SIX

ROADMAP STEP 6: OPERATIONS

A few weeks later, Greg and I gathered all the managers from the Jim Kennis stores for a follow-up meeting to review their One Page Roadmaps and set objectives for the upcoming quarter.

When I walked into the conference room where everyone was chatting and filling up coffee cups before the meeting, I was optimistic that we'd be able to get a lot done. The managers had done their work after their one-on-ones with me, and Greg had already made necessary changes to management at the stores, filled talent gaps, and now felt solid about the team moving forward.

As such, I didn't really expect that I'd need to spend the first half hour of the meeting backtracking—but I did, because almost the moment the meeting began, I realized that many of the managers had a distressing mindset: that they had already won the game, just by setting their strategy.

They'd done their one-page roadmaps. They'd completed their dealership health assessments. Everything looked clean and buttoned up. In their minds, the heavy lifting was behind them.

Before we got too far in, I said what I knew needed to be said. "I'm glad you did the work to get here," I told them. "But I need to be honest—you're not done. Getting your one-page roadmaps in place is just the beginning."

A few people raised their eyebrows. One manager chuckled under his breath, like he was thinking, *Come on… give me a break.*

I kept going. "Right now, you're in the locker room. You've gone through the game plan. You've had the team talk. But operations? That's what happens after you leave this room. It's not the plan. It's the *execution* of the plan."

I walked over to the whiteboard and wrote down a simple formula: **Operations = Execution.**

"This is where the work starts. Not ends. Next we need to talk about the operational routines that turn your strategies into wins. You don't see football teams reviewing plays once and heading out to the field thinking they've got it, right? They drill. They practice. They refine. Why would we expect less from ourselves?"

I looked around the room. They were listening now, and seemed less resistant to the message. "The strategy you built is good," I said. "But if you don't get into a daily rhythm—if you don't start moving with intention—it stays in the binder. And eventually, so does your progress."

CHAPTER SIX

EXECUTION IS EVERYTHING

The word that often gets overlooked in dealership operations, even after all the planning and strategy sessions, is *execution*.

Execution is the piece that separates theory from practice. It's where the plan either takes shape or falls apart. You can spend weeks building a thoughtful strategy—aligning goals, forecasting performance, mapping out the customer journey—but if the team doesn't follow through consistently, none of it holds. Execution is what makes the difference. It's not flashy, but it's everything.

Many organizations struggle with execution because, well, people are people. We're not machines. We're not programmable. Even with the best intentions, we drift. Distractions creep in, energy dips, and priorities shift. That's human nature. The difference between teams that struggle and teams that perform comes down to routines. Routines offer structure where it's needed most. A solid routine doesn't trap anyone—it frees them. It creates predictability, lowers stress, and makes it easier to stay focused on what matters.

In operations, routines are a form of discipline. Not in a rigid or punitive way, but in the way a personal forecast creates clarity. People sometimes think of a forecast as something restrictive, something you turn to only when things go wrong—but in reality, a forecast gives direction. It helps you decide where your money should go instead of wondering where it went.

Execution works the same way. Daily routines, consistent check-ins, and thoughtful follow-through take the strategy off the whiteboard and bring it into the real world. Forecasting only works if there's a commitment to daily execution. That's what keeps a dealership healthy—sticking with the plan long enough for it to deliver.

Execution isn't a final step. It's an ongoing practice that holds the whole thing together.

In your dealership, great execution comes down to treating each department like its own business—with standard culture and SOPs across the board, but its own business nonetheless. Yes, everyone is under one roof. Yes, it's one brand, one leadership team, one mission. But if you zoom in, each department functions almost like its own mini shop. Each has its own profit and loss statement. Its own customer touchpoints. Its own rhythms, challenges, and internal culture. That's not a problem. In fact, when it's approached with intention, it's one of the dealership's greatest strengths.

But if each department is its own business, then each one needs strong operations to run well. You can't assume that a well-run Sales department automatically means Service is humming. Or that success in F&I means administration is efficient. Every department has to be looked at on its own terms. It has to be led, supported, and optimized based on what it uniquely needs. That's where things get real.

CHAPTER SIX

A COACHING CULTURE

Execution comes from the top. If each of your departments is going to run like its own business, that means the department managers should be leading like CEOs. This goes way beyond scheduling and holding people accountable to policies. It involves building a coaching culture so that each employee can grow into their full potential and move beyond their current role.

Coaching is different from managing and leading. It requires getting close to the work and the person doing it. Coaching means walking alongside someone—helping them see what's possible, supporting them when they stumble, and celebrating progress, not just results. It's patient and personal. In a dealership, that might look like slowing down to role play a tough customer conversation, or helping an advisor understand the "why" behind a process, not just the "how." Coaching creates space for learning without judgment, which is where real development happens.

Managers who coach help their teams become more capable and more confident. Instead of always stepping in to fix something, they ask better questions and invite people to think things through. That shift changes everything. It builds resilience, reduces dependency, and helps people feel valued.

Here are two major ways all dealership and department managers can step into the coaching role:

1. **The daily huddle:** A meeting that brings everyone together to align on objectives and culture, every day.
2. **Roleplaying scenarios:** Throw out the scripts and help employees practice Right Action in controlled sessions.

THE DAILY HUDDLE

One of the first things I ask in any organization is, "How often do you meet?"

The answer tells you more than a schedule ever could. Most of the time, there isn't a formal daily huddle in place. There might be conversations throughout the day, people checking in briefly, talking in passing, solving problems on the fly. From the outside, that might seem like enough. The team seems busy and communication is happening. But underneath that activity, something important is missing.

Those conversations—quick, unstructured, often rushed—are like ships passing in the night. People talk, but they don't align. There's no dedicated space to step back, look at the big picture, and ask the right questions: *How are we doing? Where are we stuck? What do we need to do next?* Many teams resist creating that space. The reason is almost always time. There's a belief that they can't afford to pause, even briefly, to meet on purpose. What often happens instead is rework. They lose time fixing problems that could have been avoided with a few minutes of clear, shared direction.

CHAPTER SIX

Some teams push back and suggest a *weekly* meeting. On paper, that sounds reasonable. One meeting to look back and plan ahead. But here's what happens. Say you meet on a Monday and review the week before. You identify a problem that's been affecting performance—and now that problem has been going on for seven days. If you don't take action until after that meeting, it could take another week to fully resolve. That delay creates unnecessary risk.

Again, in a dealership, cash is king, and time is directly tied to money. Delaying an operational fix by a week can mean tens of thousands of dollars in lost gross profit. That's why high-performing dealerships meet daily. They use those huddles to track the flow of cash, protect it, and respond to issues in real time. It's not just a meeting. It's one of the most effective ways to take care of the business.

The daily huddle is one of the simplest tools a dealership can use to build clarity, connection, and momentum, but it's also one of the most misunderstood. Too often, it turns into a rushed status update or a glorified to-do list. When that happens, you miss the real power of the huddle. Because at its best, the daily huddle is a manager's best chance to lead, coach, and connect with their team every single day.

To do that well, you have to be clear on roles. Managers manage processes. Leaders lead people. Coaches walk side by side with both. All three are necessary. They aren't titles; they're functions. And depending on the day—or even the hour—the same person might be called to play all three roles.

In the huddle, those distinctions matter. A manager might use the huddle to check on metrics, the Critical Number, and sales progress. *Where do we stand with our pending deals? When are they going to get delivered? What's the next step with those customers that didn't buy yesterday, and what is the next step to get the deal closed?* That's important, because it creates accountability.

But if that's all the huddle does, you're only managing; you're not leading, and you're definitely not coaching.

Leadership in the huddle sounds different. It's less about tasks and more about tone. Leaders use the huddle to remind people what matters and why, in order to reinforce the cultural values that drive the work. Even if it's just a quick reflection or a shout-out to someone who went above and beyond yesterday, it shapes the emotional and cultural tone of the day.

If all the key department heads gathered in a daily huddle every morning, there would be no mystery about what's happening across the store. Everyone would know where the pressure points are. They'd know what needs attention and what's working well. The daily huddle also creates shared awareness, which becomes the foundation for meaningful action.

Without that daily rhythm, things tend to unravel. Communication becomes reactive. Problems get caught too late, and departments fall out of sync. Without a structured huddle, the whole operation leans toward chaos. A few minutes each morning can make

CHAPTER SIX

the difference between managing the day and being managed by it.

Picture this daily routine: every day in the huddle, each salesperson is assigned a set number of parking spots on the used car lot. If there are 100 cars in inventory and 10 salespeople, then each one is responsible for 10 vehicles. After the huddle, salespeople walk to their assigned spots. They check that each car is clean, the tires are inflated, the stickers are accurate, and everything is frontline ready. Then they earn a small stipend if one of their assigned cars sells, regardless of who closed the deal.

If you had that process in place for Sales, you could virtually guarantee that every piece of inventory on the lot was always in top sales condition. Expand that thinking to the rest of your departments, and you can see how daily routines and attention to detail spread to a wider culture of care and attention that would take any dealership from functional to exceptional.

ROLEPLAYING SCENARIOS

Daily coaching is where the huddle can become truly transformative. One of the most practical ways to coach inside a dealership is through daily role play.

In a well-run dealership, every department operates like its own business. And if that's true, then every department also needs someone playing the role of a sales manager, someone whose job is to coach, support, and help their team close the loop between opportunity and action.

Let's take the service department. Too often, we see the service manager as purely operational, focused on scheduling, efficiency, and problem-solving. But that view is too narrow. If we want the service team to drive results, then the service manager needs to function more like a floor manager on the sales side.

Picture this: A customer brings their car in for service. The advisor reviews the technician's inspection, then walks the customer through the recommended work. Some of those recommendations get approved. Others don't. The customer declines a repair or a service, maybe with a polite, "Thanks, not today." That's where the service manager steps in—not to pressure, but to engage.

Just like a floor manager might approach a customer in the showroom and say, "Hey, I know there are a few things you're considering. What's holding you back from moving forward now?" The service manager can ask the same kind of question to understand the customer better. "Is it timing? Is it budget? Is there something you need more clarity on?"

In this model, the service advisor is the salesperson. The service manager is the person who helps the advisor navigate the moments when a customer is hesitating, and guides them to a decision that makes sense for the customer and for the business.

It also means that the service manager, like a sales manager, is responsible for regular, structured coaching. This is where the morning huddle is a coaching opportunity. What challenges are

CHAPTER SIX

your advisors facing? What conversations are stalling? What support do they need to confidently guide customers through the service process? Create daily role plays around each of these and make it a routine.

Daily role play gives employees a safe place to practice the conversations that matter. How do you present a repair recommendation with confidence? How do you handle objections without getting defensive? How do you turn a frustrated customer into a loyal one?

These aren't "soft" skills; they're business-critical capabilities. And they get stronger with repetition, feedback, and the supervision of an invested coach.

Because every single department in the dealership not only interacts with customers in some way, but also upholds the business's culture, there is no department that wouldn't benefit from regular practice in cultural standards.

OPERATIONS DEPARTMENT BY DEPARTMENT

The hallmark of great operations in any department is consistency, clarity, and connection. You can feel it when you walk in. People know what they're doing and why. They understand how their role connects to the larger goals of the department and the dealership as a whole. Expectations are clear, systems are in place, and communication flows freely. Those aren't accidental outcomes. They're signs of intentional operational leadership.

All of this is possible, but none of it happens automatically. It requires leadership at every level that sees each department not just as a piece of the whole, but as a business in its own right. A business with people, processes, outcomes, and culture. When we treat it that way—when we give each department the operational care and clarity it needs—we don't just build stronger departments. We build a stronger dealership. One that runs with intention. One where people can thrive. One where the customer feels the difference the moment they walk in.

Let's walk through each department and the roadmap for operations they should be driving toward.

NEW VEHICLE DEPARTMENT

In the new vehicle department, operational excellence hinges on discipline, collaboration, and speed. It's not enough to simply have cars on the lot. The goal is to have the *right* cars—at the right time, in the right condition, ready to be seen, driven, and sold. That takes more than good instincts. It takes strong systems, thoughtful relationships, and a real sense of urgency.

Inventory management in new vehicles has to be tight. This is not a department where you can afford to be loose or reactive. The financial stakes are high. Vehicles that sit too long hurt your

CHAPTER SIX

floorplan and tie up capital. Vehicles that are poorly matched to your market don't move, no matter how many incentives you stack on top. So the inventory strategy has to be both data-driven and demand-aware. You need visibility into what's selling, what's stalling, and what's coming. And you need to make decisions based on facts, not feelings.

Great inventory management in this department is both strong and stringent. Every incoming unit is planned for. There's a clear rationale for why it was ordered and how it fits into the broader sales strategy. It's not just about what the manufacturer is offering; it's about what the market is absorbing. The sales team knows what's inbound. The marketing team is looped in. And there's regular communication across roles to make sure the entire front-end operation is ready to act when those vehicles land.

And then there's the manufacturer relationship. This is not optional. It's essential. There is an obligation to purchase a certain number of vehicles, and that obligation isn't just a line item. It's a partnership. When that relationship is strong—when there's consistent, transparent communication between the dealership and the manufacturer or distributor—everything runs more smoothly. Allocations are more strategic. Support is easier to access. And challenges can be addressed early, not after they've impacted your bottom line.

This kind of collaboration doesn't just happen. It takes intentional effort. It means staying proactive in your communications.

Providing feedback. Asking for support when needed. And keeping your team aligned with what's coming next. Because this isn't just about filling a lot—it's about planning an inventory that turns.

That leads directly to the next operational priority: cycle time. In new vehicles, speed matters. The goal is to shrink the time between acquisition and front-line readiness as much as possible. The minute a vehicle lands, the clock starts ticking. How fast can it be inspected, detailed, photographed, priced, and merchandised? How quickly can it be live on the website and ready for a test drive?

The most effective new vehicle departments treat this process like a relay race. There's no dead space between handoffs. Everyone knows their role. The get-ready team is ready; the digital team is notified; the sales managers are tracking progress. Every delay—no matter how small—adds up. So the best stores create clear expectations and tight workflows to keep the process moving without compromising quality.

When you get all of this right—inventory discipline, manufacturer collaboration, and fast cycle time—you create a new vehicle department that performs like a machine. It becomes a driver of profit, a source of energy on the floor, and a place where customers experience the kind of confidence and clarity that turns one-time buyers into long-term relationships.

CHAPTER SIX

USED VEHICLE DEPARTMENT

The used vehicle department is one of the most dynamic and high-stakes areas of the dealership. It moves fast, changes often, and demands constant attention. Unlike new vehicles, where pricing and availability are largely driven by the manufacturer, used vehicles live in the real-time marketplace. It's fluid. It's competitive. And if you're not strategic about how you operate, it's easy to fall behind.

One of the things that makes an operation strong is having clear, consistent, and actionable processes—and as we discussed in the last chapter, it's surprising how often it gets overlooked. A lot of teams have an unspoken sense of how things *should* go, but those processes aren't always written down. And if they're not written, they're not being executed the same way every time. That gap shows up in ways you can feel. Miscommunication, missed steps, and inconsistent experiences all add up.

The used vehicle department brings this into focus. On the surface, it might seem similar to new vehicles, but there's one big difference. The dealer gets to decide how big they want that department to be. There's no outside manufacturer dictating volume. That autonomy gives the store a lot of power, but it also puts the responsibility squarely on their shoulders.

If a dealer wants to move 100 used vehicles a month, they'll need to stock enough inventory to support that. If they want to hit

1,000, the scale and systems have to match. It's a choice. And once that choice is made, the real work begins—because managing that inventory well is what determines whether the operation thrives or stalls out.

Inventory management matters everywhere, but in used vehicles, it matters even more. The dealership owns those cars. There's no safety net. Every dollar spent is tied up in metal sitting on the lot. And if that metal sits too long, it starts costing more than it's worth.

This plays out in other industries, too. I've seen marina owners hold onto used boats for a year, sometimes even two. That inventory ties up cash. It takes up space. And boats don't get better with age, especially when they're sitting outside. The longer they sit, the less they're worth. That principle holds true whether it's a boat, a car, a motorcycle, an ATV, or any other used asset.

So you have to decide: what kind of used vehicle department do you want to have? What size makes sense for your market, your capacity, your team? Once you've got clarity on that, the next step is speed—specifically, cycle time. The goal is to move each vehicle from acquisition to front-line ready in the shortest time possible.

Every day a car sits in limbo is a day you're paying for it without getting anything back. That's where well-documented processes make all the difference. If your team knows exactly what happens when a car is acquired—who touches it, when, how, and why—then you've got a fighting chance of hitting that short cycle time.

CHAPTER SIX

If everyone's improvising or waiting for someone else to move first, then things stall. And once they stall, they don't just fix themselves.

The hallmark of a high-performing used vehicle department is speed and precision. The goal is to turn inventory every 30 days. Not just a few units; the *entire* inventory. That kind of discipline requires a completely different mindset. Used vehicles aren't meant to sit. Every day they age, they lose value. So if a vehicle is still on the lot after 45 or 60 days, it's not just a slow seller. It's a liability.

This is where cycle time becomes critical. The most effective used vehicle departments get cars from acquisition to front-line ready in 72 hours or less. That means the vehicle is cleaned, inspected, reconditioned, photographed, and merchandised—fast. There's no dragging feet. No waiting around for approvals. Everyone involved in the process knows the timeline and moves with urgency. Every hour counts, because the faster a car is retail-ready, the sooner it can start generating interest and moving toward a sale.

But speed alone isn't enough. Pricing strategy is just as important. The used vehicle department has to operate with a firm commitment to market pricing. That means always selling at the price the market supports, not the price that feels good or looks nice on paper. This isn't about margin. It's about velocity. Price the car where it needs to be to move, not where you wish it would sell.

Great stores use dynamic pricing. Think of it like the price of gas—it changes based on supply, demand, and what competitors are doing. You don't set a price once and walk away. You revisit it daily. You adjust. You react to what's happening in your market. That might mean dropping the price of a slow mover after seven days. Or raising the price on a unit that's suddenly in high demand. It's not emotional. It's strategic. The data leads the way.

That same mindset applies to acquisition. In a fast-turn environment, you don't buy in bulk. You buy in small, intentional batches. You stay nimble. That allows you to adjust based on what's selling, what's sitting, and what the market is telling you. It keeps inventory fresh and relevant. And it helps you avoid the trap of trying to sell cars the market no longer wants.

But before you buy anything, there's a more fundamental question that needs to be answered: What's your market differentiator? Do you want to dominate the under-$20,000 price point? Do you want to be known for nearly-new certified pre-owned vehicles? Do you specialize in trucks? Imports? SUVs? There is no one-size-fits-all approach. But there *is* a wrong approach, and it's trying to be everything to everyone. The best used car departments are built with intention. They know their lane, and they stay in it. That clarity drives every decision—what to buy, how to price it, and who to market it to.

All of this—every decision, every process—points to one goal: turn cars fast, price them right, and serve the customer with clarity and confidence. When the used vehicle department runs with this level of operational discipline, it doesn't just add to the dealership's bottom line; it becomes a growth engine for the organization.

CHAPTER SIX

SERVICE & PARTS DEPARTMENTS

The service department is at the heart of the dealership's long-term success, and it's all about the relationship with the customer. A well-operated service department builds trust, drives retention, and creates consistent revenue. But for all that potential, they only work when operations are strong—especially in the small, daily details that shape the customer experience.

One of the most important operational levers in service is appointment scheduling—or *reservation* scheduling. To get your team into the upscale service mindset, I encourage you to start calling "appointments" reservations.

Scheduling seems simple on the surface. A customer calls or goes online, picks a time, and shows up. But in reality, how you schedule reservations sets the tone for the entire day, both for the customer and for your team.

Effective scheduling starts with respect for capacity. Overbooking might seem like a way to get more through the shop, but it almost always backfires. When you cram too many cars into one day, you create stress for your advisors, overwhelm your technicians, and disappoint your customers. What looked like a busy, productive day quickly turns into a scramble. Timelines slip. Communication breaks down. And customers start to feel like they're just a number.

The better approach is to schedule with intention. That means leaving time open for walk-ins and emergencies. It means planning for variability, not hoping everything runs perfectly. Because things *will* come up. A check engine light. A tow-in. A regular customer who couldn't plan ahead. If your schedule is already maxed out, those unexpected moments become problems. But if you've left space, they become opportunities to show up, serve well, and build trust.

And this leads directly into one of the most overlooked parts of the service experience: the advisor-customer interaction. The meet and greet. The walkaround. The moment of real human connection. Too often, this gets rushed or skipped entirely. The common excuse? "We don't have time." But the truth is, this moment is part of the work. It's not optional. It's not extra. It's essential.

That's why the best-run service departments have an *executable, written process* for how advisors meet, greet, and work with their customers. It's not about being robotic. It's about being reliable. Every customer gets the same quality of attention. The same care. The same thoughtful questions and clear communication. That consistency builds confidence.

Think of it through the lens of *know, like, trust, try*. When advisors take the time to engage with customers—genuinely, patiently, respectfully—they build relationships. The customer gets to *know* the advisor. Maybe even *like* them. Over time, they begin to *trust* them. And when a recommendation is made, the customer is far more likely to *try* it.

CHAPTER SIX

Here's where scheduling and process intersect. That walkaround? That relationship-building conversation? It takes time. If the day is overbooked and the advisor is running from one drop-off to the next, there's no space for it. That's not a personal failing. That's an operational one. If we want advisors to show up with presence, care, and consistency, we have to give them the space to do it.

Great service and parts departments don't happen by accident. They're the result of clear systems, thoughtful scheduling, and a culture that values quality over chaos. When you schedule with care, build in time for the unexpected, and support your advisors with structured, repeatable processes, you create a service experience that customers actually *want* to come back to.

ROUTINES SET YOU FREE

The bottom line with successful operations is setting and committing to successful routines. The most successful dealerships I have worked with have mastered this element more than any other.

And yet so often I talk with dealers and managers who believe that routines like a daily huddle are too constraining for their employees. They'd rather just, to use a football analogy, "let their employees run the ball."

I love that analogy because it's the best way to illustrate why routines are actually the only way to win. Imagine you saved up and bought your whole family tickets to watch your home team play in the Super Bowl. You lay out thousands of dollars, maybe you travel a couple hours to the stadium, and you wait in interminably long lines before finally settling into your seats in a packed stadium.

Then the game begins, and your team runs out onto the field and snaps the ball without a huddle.

If this ever happened, the entire stadium would be in shock. Every team huddles before nearly every play. They take a moment to regroup, get aligned, call the play, and make sure everyone knows what's coming next. Without that pause, they'd fall apart. The game would unravel. So why do we accept that kind of discipline on the field but resist it in our organizations? What makes us think our teams can function without the same level of clarity?

Daily huddles are the glue that holds operations together. They're the space where your strategy turns into execution. They help teams move beyond vague alignment into real, coordinated action.

Similarly, roleplaying scenarios is the same as a football team running drills at practice. A coach would never just tell their players what the game plan is and leave it to them to remember on the field. No, they run drills over and over again in practice so that when the time comes to run the lay for real, nothing is left to chance.

It's one thing to say, "We did our strategic planning. We built the one-page roadmap. We talked to every department head."

CHAPTER SIX

That's all important, and it lays the groundwork.

But making a game plan is not the same as running the plays. Strategy happens in the locker room; execution is getting out on the field and doing what you said you were going to do. It's where the planning ends and the real movement begins.

Operational routines make that possible. They allow your entire organization to practice, adjust, and show up with purpose.

KEY TAKEAWAYS ON OPERATIONS

Here are five key takeaways from this chapter:

1. **Execution only matters when it's consistent.** Creating a strategy is just the beginning—real progress only happens when that strategy is executed daily through structured routines.

2. **Departments must operate like individual businesses.** Each department has its own needs, challenges, and rhythm, and each must be led and coached intentionally for the dealership to perform as a whole.

3. **Coaching is what turns managers into leaders.** Daily huddles and roleplaying scenarios provide a reliable rhythm for managers to guide,

support, and develop their teams.

4. **Routines create freedom and clarity.** When daily structures like huddles and training drills are in place, teams waste less time, solve problems faster, and stay aligned on what matters.

5. **Execution holds your culture together.** The way people show up, communicate, and follow through on commitments determines whether your culture lives in practice or stays stuck on paper.

CHAPTER SEVEN

ROADMAP STEP 7: REVENUE

It was just after noon at Jim Kennis Automotive, and we were about halfway through the manager meeting. The morning had gone well. The team was engaged, the energy was strong, and people seemed to be settling into a groove with their planning.

During the lunch break, I was grabbing coffee in the corner of the room when I overheard one of the managers talking about the sales department at his store. He was proud—rightfully so—about the number of units his team had moved that month. It was a solid number. A win, by most standards. He was listing them off like stats on a scoreboard: truck, SUV, another SUV, sedan, crossover.

I walked over and asked him, "How many of those units have families who also might be in the market for a vehicle?"

He paused. "Oh," he said, a little caught off guard. "We don't really track that kind of stuff."

I nodded, thanked him, and let the moment pass. But I knew exactly what I needed to say after lunch.

Once everyone settled back in, I stood up and said, "I heard something earlier that I think speaks to the mindset shift we need to make if we want to stop chasing monthly wins and start building long-term revenue growth."

I looked around the room.

"We're counting units. And that's good. But that's not the whole picture. A sale isn't a single transaction. It's an introduction to a network. Every vehicle that leaves this lot is connected to a household, a circle of people, a group of potential future customers. And if we're not paying attention to that, we're leaving money on the table every single day."

I let it sit for a second. No one reached for their water bottle.

"You're not just in the business of moving metal. You're in the business of relationships. If you sold a vehicle to someone last week and you don't know whether they've got another vehicle in the driveway, or a teenager who's about to start driving, or a neighbor who was helping them shop—you're leaving opportunity behind."

There were some quiet nods.

"I know it's easy to look at the board at the end of the month and count how many units you moved. But if you're not thinking about how many people each of those units connects you to, you're missing the multiplier. You're selling in a straight line, when you could be selling in a circle."

I stepped back toward the table and added, "You want to grow your revenue? Shift your mindset. Start asking better questions after the sale. Start looking past the numbers. Build the kind of

CHAPTER SEVEN

follow-up systems that keep those connections alive. That's where the future is."

In this chapter, I'm not going to give you a quick three- or five-step action plan for increasing sales—because one doesn't exist.

Instead, I'll guide you through what really needs to happen in your dealership in order to make a real impact on sales: a complete shift in this idea of what sales even *is*, and the role of a salesperson in a highly successful long-term dealership vision.

THE NEW SALES REALITY

"The problem is simple: not enough sales."

That's the conversation at nearly every dealership right now. Leadership wants more volume, more consistency, more traction in a market that feels harder than it should. And it's not because the desire for growth is new. All dealerships want more sales—always have. More sales produce more cash. Cash, the oxygen of the business, fuels everything else: service, parts, trade-ins, retention. Sales build the long-term health of the store. They bring customers back for service, drive future trades, and keep the whole ecosystem alive.

What we're seeing now is a sharp contrast to what the industry experienced just a few years ago. COVID disrupted everything. Inventory tightened. In many stores, profitability soared even though sales volume dropped. There was a psychological shift; customers knew supply was limited, so urgency went through the roof. It wasn't about comparison shopping. It was about getting *any* vehicle at all.

With fewer units on the ground and less need for advertising, overhead expenses dropped. Interest rates were lower. Cars were selling themselves. It created an environment where dealerships didn't need the same intensity of effort, and yet the results were extraordinary. For many salespeople, especially those who entered the industry during this window, it felt like success came easily. They closed deals without having to navigate objections, compete on value, or build long-term trust. For a while, that worked.

Then reality hit. By the end of 2023, it was becoming clear that the market was shifting. Sales volume wasn't recovering as quickly as hoped. Inventory levels were improving, but customer urgency had cooled. By 2024, many dealerships found themselves facing one of the hardest years in recent memory. That easy profitability disappeared, and the skills gap that had been masked by the boom started to show.

A lot of people in sales had early wins during the high tide. It felt good. It felt like they were made for the job. The challenge is, many didn't go deeper after those first few wins. They were willing to put in more hours, take more ups, push harder—but they weren't always willing to build new skills. They didn't study the craft. They didn't practice conversations or sharpen their product knowledge. The goal was still to sell more, but the path to mastery felt like something extra rather than something essential.

CHAPTER SEVEN

This moment is asking for something different. Selling in today's market takes more than grit. It takes skill. It takes patience. It takes people who are willing to get curious again, to ask better questions, to really learn what it means to build trust. Sales volume will recover. It always does. The question is, who will be ready when it does? The ones who learn to master the craft now will be the ones who thrive—not just in the next cycle, but for the long haul.

DON'T JUST SELL—BECOME A MASTER OF THE CRAFT

The solution isn't complicated, but it does require a mindset shift.

It starts with agility. Yes, as we've discussed previously, you absolutely need a sales process. A strong, repeatable process creates structure and gives your team something to lean on. But the process, on its own, does not make sales. *People* make sales. To other people. That means relationships come first. Curiosity, empathy, attention—those are the things that build trust and move people from hesitation to action.

This market doesn't leave much room for being stuck. You need to be agile. That means knowing when something isn't working and having the courage to adjust. If the numbers are flat, if traffic is down, if people aren't following up—it's not enough to work harder. You have to work smarter. You have to try something new. Every day you delay, you're leaving opportunities behind. Maybe that means offering remote sales options. Maybe it means texting instead of calling. Maybe it means reworking your approach entirely. The goal is not to change just for the sake of change, but to respond to what people actually need right now.

Salespeople who succeed today are students of the craft. They don't wait for motivation to show up. They live and breathe sales. They want to get better because they care about helping people. They see their work as service. A great salesperson connects, listens, and adapts; they meet people where they are. That is mastery—not some secret script or clever closing line, but the daily practice of caring enough to do it well.

This kind of selling is personalized. It's flexible. It meets customers on their terms. You learn how each person wants to buy, and then you meet them there. For one person, it's sitting down in person and walking through every number. For someone else, it's texting back and forth until they're ready to commit. You're always on duty, whether you're at your desk, walking the lot, or answering a quick question that turns into something bigger.

We're in a very particular moment, and part of the solution is letting go of the habits that worked during a time of abundance but are now holding people back. There's still a lingering sense in many stores that the patterns from 2020 and 2021 will somehow still apply. That stretch of time changed the way we operated, and

CHAPTER SEVEN

in some ways, we're still untangling the aftereffects. When inventory was tight and customers were bidding up vehicles, it created a false sense of ease. Sales were happening quickly, often with less effort, and that shaped behaviors that are no longer helping. Now the tide has turned. It's no longer feast—it's famine. And that shift requires a different kind of awareness, a different kind of effort.

Part of what makes this so tricky is that many people haven't adjusted yet. They're still working off assumptions that no longer fit the current landscape. The idea that sales will come just because the doors are open doesn't hold anymore. People have more choices, more hesitations, and more need for genuine service. That means every interaction counts. If a customer calls the store and gets a one-word answer or gets passed off without care, they won't wait around. They'll call the next dealership, and you've lost the opportunity. That's the reality. It's not just about who's on the floor or who's assigned to sales. It's about how the entire team shows up.

In this moment, every person in the dealership is part of the sales team, whether it says so on their name tag or not. In fact, even teams *outside* of the dealership, like the Business Development Center and the website team, are part of the sales team. That doesn't mean everyone has to close deals. It means everyone contributes to the experience that leads to trust, follow-up, and eventually, a sale. If someone calls or walks in, whoever picks up the phone or greets them at the door is the sales team at that moment. How they show up—how present, helpful, and informed they are—can make or break the entire relationship. That shift in thinking is where real progress begins.

OWNING YOUR MARKET

Unless you're in a market where the population is declining or the consumer base has fundamentally changed, people are still buying. They're still spending on products and services. So the question is, if they're not buying from you, why not? That's where the real conversation begins. It's easy to point to the economy or interest rates or competition. But at the heart of it, the challenge is often more local—and more personal—than that.

Most dealerships do not own their local market, and that's a significant problem. If you're a Honda dealer, for example, you should be the first and only place people think of in your area when it's time to buy a Honda. That's what owning your market means. But instead, many stores use what could best be described as a "buckshot" approach to advertising. They spread their message far and wide—across counties, regions, even states—hoping to catch someone's attention. In very rural areas, that can make sense. People will travel long distances because they have to. In suburban or urban areas, though, it creates more noise than connection. You might pull in someone from 100 miles away who thinks they're getting a great deal, but you'll never see them again. There's no relationship, no loyalty, no long-term value.

CHAPTER SEVEN

The real opportunity lies in focusing on the geographic footprint you can actually serve well. That means investing in the people around you. Offering pick-up and drop-off service. Providing shuttle options. Making it easy for people in your community to say, "I don't need to go anywhere else." The lifetime value of a customer is enormous. It's never just one vehicle. It's repeat sales, service reservations, parts, referrals, trade-ins. Most people don't *want* to go to ten different dealerships. They want to have someone they trust. Someone they can call and say, "It's time—what can you get me into?" The dealership wants that kind of relationship, too. Loyalty works both ways.

Most of the opportunities in a dealership don't come from the customers who buy on the first visit. They come from the customers who *don't*. Those are the people most stores ignore without meaning to. If someone walks in, or calls, or clicks through to a digital lead form, they're reaching out with some kind of need. If your only focus is on the one person who's ready to buy *right now*, then you're missing the much bigger picture. Every lead is a moment of connection. If you answer the phone or respond to a chat, you're the sales team at that moment.

Many stores track customer retention, and in the automotive world, some hover around 65 percent. That might sound like a solid number at first glance. But look closer. That means 35 percent of your customers went somewhere else. A third of the people you worked to serve didn't come back. Why? Most of the time, it's not price—any dealership can beat someone else's deal. The issue isn't the math. It's the connection, or the lack of it. This is where salespeople get disrupted without even realizing it. They assume customers are leaving for a better offer, but often, it's because they didn't feel remembered, valued, or prioritized.

The truth is, the things that really move the needle in sales are within your control. They aren't just tied to the numbers. They come down to hard and soft skills. Listening. Following up. Making the customer experience feel seamless. Being agile enough to mold your approach to what each customer wants, instead of forcing everyone into the same process. That's what builds trust. That's what keeps people coming back. It's not a tactic. It's a mindset—and it starts the moment you decide to own your market instead of hoping someone else doesn't get there first.

SHIFTING THE ROLE OF SALESPERSON

If there's one thing everyone wants in a dealership, it's a quick fix. When sales slow down or margins tighten, the natural impulse is to look for something fast—some new tactic, some shortcut, some miracle strategy that promises results without the wait.

But quick fixes rarely last. Sustainable growth takes longer. It takes more intention, more patience, and more trust in the process. That's true in life, and it's definitely true in sales. You can't drop

CHAPTER SEVEN

thirty pounds overnight. You can't rebuild momentum by next Monday. What you *can* do is start showing up differently tomorrow—smarter, more connected, more focused on the long game.

If you want to solve the problem and build something that lasts, it starts with a shift in how you see the role of a salesperson. Salespeople often focus entirely on the transaction, but that's only part of the picture. A better question to ask is this: do you know everything about every customer you've sold to? Do you know what other vehicles they own? Where they service them? Who in their household might be the next driver?

If you want to build a real relationship, those questions matter. Sales is no longer about being "their car guy" for one sale. It's about being *their* person—the person they call when they need help with anything related to transportation. Not just for today's deal, but for whatever comes next.

That kind of relationship doesn't end at the sale. It deepens afterward. One way to do that is by creating stronger connections between sales and service. In most dealerships, the salesperson has no idea when their customer is coming in for a service reservation. They're completely out of the loop, even though the data exists. The CRM knows. The customer gets reminders. But the person who sold them the car? Often, they don't know at all. Imagine if that changed. Imagine if the salesperson saw that reservation on the calendar and showed up at the service lane just to say hello. Not to sell. Just to show up. That one gesture changes everything.

Now, this idea usually gets pushback. Salespeople say, "You want me to go into the shop when I have other things to do?" They resist it because they don't see the long-term value.

But this *is* the long-term value. This is how you build a dealership that grows no matter what the market is doing. It's how you stay connected to the customer, so that five years from now, they're still calling *you*—not shopping around for someone else. This approach isn't about flooding the top of the funnel. It's about taking care of what you already have. And it's about recognizing that if you're spending a fortune on advertising but not doing *this* kind of relationship work, you're missing one of the most valuable growth opportunities in the store.

Here's what happens that most people don't see: when someone brings home a new vehicle—whether it's a car, a truck, a boat, or an ATV—everyone around them notices. Friends know. Family members know. Neighbors know. In that one sale, you've touched an entire network.

Now imagine a salesperson who sells fifteen vehicles a month; that's 180 in a year. Let's say each of those customers knows just five people who might also be in the market. That's 900 additional opportunities, right there. Now, even if you're 80 percent wrong—even if only a fraction of those actually convert—that's still a significant number of sales. Maybe 40. Maybe 60. And that's just in year one. Keep going, and the numbers start to multiply. It doesn't take long for that compounding effect to turn a good year into a

CHAPTER SEVEN

career-defining one. Not by accident, but by design.

Many salespeople don't chase that kind of growth because it requires a different mindset. It's slower. It takes time. It requires you to be intentional long after the sale is closed. You're not just selling a product; you're building a network. That means checking in after delivery. Asking about other vehicles in the household. Keeping an eye on service visits. Knowing when a customer might be ready for a trade. Most salespeople don't want to go down that road. It takes effort. It takes patience, stepping away from the instant gratification of the "what's in front of me" sale and investing in something much bigger. But this is where real success lives.

This long-term approach is not flashy or dramatic. It's built in quiet moments—remembering a customer's daughter just got her license, noticing when someone's lease is coming due, offering help without asking for anything in return. It's not about knowing how to close. It's about knowing how to care. That care builds loyalty, reputation, and turns a business built on volume into a business built on trust.

Dealerships pour millions into advertising every year, casting a wide net and hoping to catch the right buyers. It's what some call the "buckshot" approach—spread the message as far as possible and see who responds. But the truth is, many stores don't know who their best customers are. They haven't taken the time to look inward, to mine the value that already exists in their own database. These aren't Mona Lisas we're selling. The vehicle might not be one of a kind—but the relationship can be.

So yes, there's resistance. There's the argument that it takes too much time, that everyone's already too busy. That there are targets to hit this month, this week, today. But those quick wins don't stack up. They don't compound. Like chasing interest-free financing while ignoring long-term returns, they give the illusion of success without the foundation to sustain it. The disruptor is the one who's bold enough to say, "We're doing this differently." Who takes the time to ask, "Who do you know?" and then follows through. Who believes that the future of sales isn't in the product—it's in the relationship. And who is willing to build that, one conversation at a time.

What we're really talking about is shifting the mindset. Sales isn't just about closing deals; it's about building relationships. Not one-and-done interactions, but ongoing conversations that span years, vehicles, and life stages. If a salesperson focuses only on the value of the current sale, they miss the much greater value of the relationship. That relationship will include multiple sales, multiple service visits, and multiple chances to show up and make it easy for the customer to say, "I'm staying here." Every sale becomes a stepping stone, not a finish line.

When that mindset becomes the norm, everything else starts to align—loyalty, retention, reputation, and growth that doesn't depend on the market being perfect. It just depends on how you show up.

CHAPTER SEVEN

KEY TAKEAWAYS ON REVENUE

Here are five key takeaways from this chapter:

1. **Build relationships, not just transactions.** Every sale connects you to a broader network of future opportunities, and long-term success depends on nurturing those relationships beyond the initial deal.

2. **Mastery matters more than momentum.** The COVID sales environment created shortcuts that don't hold up in today's market, and sustainable growth now depends on skilled, intentional, customer-centered sales practices.

3. **Agility is the new advantage.** Salespeople who adapt quickly, stay curious, and meet customers where they are will outperform those who cling to outdated methods or rely on effort alone.

4. **Everyone in the dealership is on the sales team.** Regardless of role, every person shapes the customer's experience, and their interactions directly impact trust, loyalty, and future revenue.

5. **Owning your market starts with loyalty, not leads.** Instead of casting a wide net, the most successful dealerships focus on serving their

local customers with excellence, building a base that returns again and again.

CHAPTER EIGHT

ROADMAP STEP 8: MARKETING

By the time we wrapped up the manager meeting that day at Jim Kennis Automotive, something had majorly clicked.

I could tell by the energy of the managers as they walked out of the conference room to return to their stores. They were fired up and ready to execute for the long haul; there was a new air of confidence around each of them. This wasn't just a group of people excited by new ideas. This was now a seasoned team of experts armed with the knowledge and experience to grow their stores far beyond their previous expectations.

Once they'd all departed, Greg and I turned to a larger discussion. "I wanted to make sure we were solid in each of the stores, with the right people, the right strategy, and the right execution. Now that we have that, I'd love to get your insight on where we should put the marketing forecast for the entire company," he said.

It was news to me that Greg was considering any kind of big marketing spend this early in his tenure. "Before we go anywhere, tell me—what's your message?" I asked.

He paused. I could tell he hadn't been expecting that question. "We've got the forecast," he said. "We're planning to invest millions of dollars over the next two years."

I held my hand up. "That's great. But if you don't know exactly what you want people to believe about this group, what makes you different, why they should care—then it doesn't matter how much you spend. We'll just end up amplifying the noise."

He nodded slowly. "So we're not there yet."

"No," I said. "You're not."

Here's what I know from doing this for a long time: the majority of dealerships are stuck in the same cycle. They talk about price. Inventory. Service. They use the same language, run the same sales, rely on the same tired taglines. When everyone's shouting "we've got the best deals," no one actually stands out.

Greg didn't argue. "So we're not differentiated in the marketplace."

"Exactly," I said. "You can't spend your way into clarity. You've got to earn it first."

He took a breath. "So what do we do?"

"We back up," I told him. "We figure out what you want to be known for. Not across the whole industry, just right here—where your stores are. What do your people believe in? What do your customers need to hear? What are you offering that no one else is willing to commit to?"

In this chapter, you're going to learn exactly why most deal-

CHAPTER EIGHT

erships struggle to differentiate themselves in a crowded marketplace—and how you can make sure you're delivering exactly the message your customers want to hear.

WHAT IS YOUR MESSAGE?

The challenge many dealerships face today isn't just about inventory or pricing or customer traffic. Too many teams are working without a clear, defined, and compelling message.

When that message is missing, everything else starts to feel a little scattered, like a radio station that can't quite tune into its own frequency.

Without a strong message, it's hard to build trust. It's hard to attract the right customers, the right team members, and even the right partners. You might have all the right tools and a solid game plan, but if your message isn't cutting through the noise, you're playing with one hand tied behind your back. It's not enough to say you want to be "the best" or "the biggest" or "number one in the region." That's not a message; that's a placeholder.

A real message tells people who you are. It tells them what matters to you. It gives your employees something to stand behind and your customers something to believe in. It connects your operations to your values. And when you get it right, it makes everything else easier: sales, service, hiring, and culture.

To get there, you have to be willing to take a clear-eyed look at what the market actually needs. That gap between what a dealership is saying and what the market is asking for is where opportunity lives, and that's where your dealership can differentiate. Not by adding more words or louder ads, but by finding a message that resonates so deeply, people know it's yours the second they hear it.

A great message is crystal clear. It doesn't waffle or drift; it knows who it's talking to and what it's promising. You can feel the confidence in it. That kind of clarity doesn't just come from a lucky stroke of branding; it comes from knowing who they are and why they exist, and making that message central to every touchpoint.

For example, Tasca Automotive Group, headquartered in Rhode Island, is an example that proves the power of a message that sticks. Their tagline is "You will be satisfied." It's simple and direct; a customer knows exactly what they're getting. When the company went with that message, they didn't try to be clever. Instead, they simply chose to be clear. Over time, that clarity has built trust enormous trust with the market—Tasca has been in business and a leader in their market for over eighty years.

When your message is clear, it becomes a kind of internal compass. It helps you make decisions faster, gives your people a shared language, and reinforces the kind of experience you're trying to create, not just in theory, but in every moment and interaction.

And when your message is compelling, people remember it; they repeat it, and more importantly, they believe it. That's what makes the difference. Not a flashy slogan or a one-time campaign,

CHAPTER EIGHT

but a message that lives in your systems, your people, and your culture.

STEP 1: KNOW YOUR MARKET

There's a reason many dealerships struggle to build a compelling, differentiated message—and it's not because they lack passion or resources. It's because they don't actually know a few critical things about their customer and market.

When you don't know what you don't know, it's easy to keep doing the same thing as everyone else, hoping for different results.

Imagine a dealership in a typical market—let's call it Market A. They invest in advertising; they run campaigns, show up on social media, and print flyers. But when you line up their messages side by side with everyone else in their region, something becomes very clear.

It's all the same.

Every dealership says some version of: "We've got the best inventory. Our people are great. Our prices are the lowest. We're open all the time. Now is the best time to buy. Your trade-in will never be worth more than it is today."

It's a collection of recycled lines that sound familiar because they *are* familiar. It's the same message from dealership to dealership, repackaged with different logos and color schemes. And even though those lines might have once carried weight, now they're just white noise.

The truth is, this kind of messaging doesn't set anyone apart. It doesn't offer clarity or connection. It just blends in. Everyone ends up saying, "Me too," instead of, "Here's what makes us different."

What dealerships need to do is truly assess the needs of the market. That's the piece that often gets skipped, and the foundation that's missing.

What does this look like? It means you have to study, observe, and listen with fresh ears. You're not just guessing what the market wants—you're taking the time to understand it.

1. What are customers asking for?
2. What needs do they consistently have that aren't being met?
3. And most importantly, what needs do they have that they don't even know about?

So how do you assess the needs of an entire market from the four walls of your dealership? Simple: by talking with the customers who come in about what they need. When a customer walks in and tells you their story, read between the lines. What are they not even thinking about—but if you could provide it, they would become a customer for life? That's a good indicator of a way in which the market isn't currently being served.

CHAPTER EIGHT

STEP 2: WHO ARE YOUR COMPETITORS?

Once you've done that, the next step is to define and map your competitors. Ask these questions:
1. Who else is trying to meet these needs?
2. How are they doing it?
3. What are they missing?

Here's where it gets tricky. Most of the time, we don't actually know that much about our competitors—not really. We might have a general idea or some assumptions, but the truth is, we rarely have solid intel. And that means we have to do some reconnaissance.

It's not about spying or gaming the system; it's about doing our homework with the same level of rigor and curiosity that any serious business would bring to the table. Think about Walmart. You don't have to love them. You don't have to agree with everything they stand for. But what's undeniable is that they know what their competitors are doing. They invest in research. They watch the landscape. They stay informed.

If you want to have a complete picture of how the needs of the market are being met, and where your opportunities lie, you need to get just as informed.

STEP 3: MEET THE NEEDS OF THE MARKET

The next step is to turn that lens inward and ask, *How well are we meeting those needs?* Not in general, not according to assumptions, but in clear, specific terms.

Look at each need area individually and evaluate how effectively your dealership is delivering, in every department. Then go back and apply that same framework to your competitors. What are they doing in those same areas? How are they serving—or failing to serve—those needs?

When you see this mapped out, it starts to reveal something incredibly valuable: the gaps.

Those gaps, sometimes called the *white space* in the market, are where needs exist that nobody's meeting. Not us, not our competitors. Just open space. That's where opportunity lives. When a business identifies and steps into that white space—when they see a need and commit to filling it—they often wind up owning that corner of the market. Not for a moment, but for a stretch of time where there's no real competition in that lane. That doesn't last forever, of course. The market always adjusts. But if you get there first, you get to set the tone. You get to lead.

There's a great example of this from the automotive world. Years ago, before minivans were a thing, families had very few op-

CHAPTER EIGHT

tions. If you had a bunch of kids or needed to haul people around, you had a station wagon—big, bulky, unattractive, but functional. They got the job done.

Then someone at Chrysler asked a different question. What if there was a new kind of family vehicle? Something that wasn't a wagon, something more versatile? And in the early '80s, after years of development, Chrysler introduced the minivan. It wasn't pretty. In fact, it was objectively unattractive. But it was incredibly useful. Families could pile in, drive comfortably, and load up all the gear that life demands. The first models weren't even high-quality builds. In fact, they were rough. But it didn't matter. Nobody else was in the space.

Because Chrysler got there first, they owned the market. There was no competition—just a wide open need and one company willing to step into it.

Of course, that didn't last forever. The moment Ford and GM saw the demand, they started building their own minivans. But Chrysler had already planted their flag. Over the years, they changed hands multiple times—different ownership, different corporate structures—but the brand held on to its position. They stayed dominant because they got there early and made the space theirs.

At one point, Chrysler decided to evolve again. They introduced the four-door minivan. That single change shifted expectations across the industry. And what happened next? Everyone else followed suit. Suddenly, four-door minivans were the norm. Chrysler had led the innovation, and the rest of the market responded by saying, "Us too."

That's the power of seeing the white space clearly and moving into it with purpose. It doesn't require a perfect product. It requires vision. It requires the willingness to look past what's always been done and imagine what could be next.

The same thing happened again years later with the rise of crossovers. We had big SUVs. We had small cars. But then someone asked, *What if there was something in between?* A hybrid of space, comfort, and fuel efficiency. And today, crossovers dominate the market. They've become the default choice for a huge range of customers, simply because someone recognized a need that wasn't yet being met.

It takes the courage to look at the market with fresh eyes. But the reward is that you don't have to fight over scraps—you get to lead.

A DEEPER UNDERSTANDING

When a business truly understands its market, something interesting happens. You start to see more than just one type of customer. You begin to see patterns; you're likely serving multiple core customers, not just one big, generic group. There's usually a mainstream customer—someone who reflects the bulk of your current

CHAPTER EIGHT

base—but there's also someone else on the edge whose needs aren't being fully met by the mainstream offer.

Take electric vehicles, for example. In the beginning, EVs were pushed hard. Consumers were told they were the future. But the response wasn't quite what manufacturers had hoped. People pulled back, and adoption plateaued. What emerged was this in-between space: people didn't necessarily want a fully electric vehicle, but they were open to a hybrid, something that offered the innovation of electric without letting go of the reliability and familiarity of gas.

This is where some of the purely electric car companies misread the market. They went all in on a need they *thought* was universal. Some even lost billions in a single quarter chasing that vision. But others showed there *was* a need, even if it came at great risk early on. They built something new, broke the mold, and differentiated in a way no one else had. The lesson here isn't about being perfect—it's about seeing what others don't, or won't, and being willing to move into that space.

This concept isn't just for tech startups or electric vehicles. It applies to every segment of the auto industry. Trucks. Motorcycles. Even boats. Anytime someone identifies something unique—a white space—and builds a business around it, they gain a powerful advantage.

It all starts with a simple question: *How can we serve a market that's underserved?*

That's the heartbeat of innovation. That's where strategy begins:

not with a flashy campaign or a clever headline, but with a clear-eyed understanding of what people actually need and the courage to build something that answers it.

Truly leading in your market doesn't look like chasing what everyone else is doing, but instead, noticing what no one else is paying attention to—and building something people didn't even know they were waiting for.

THE CLEAREST MESSAGE WINS

Once you've mapped out your market and your customer needs, it's time to craft your message and build a plan around getting that message out there.

This is an area where, in my experience, dealerships struggle to find the time. They're busy. The business feels like it runs itself—people come in, they buy a car, or they go online, they buy a car. Same process, different day. And because the day-to-day keeps rolling forward, nobody stops to ask what the bigger picture should look like.

So when it comes to marketing, they rely on the usual rhythms. In December, it's the winter service push: make sure your tires are ready, check your wiper blades, get your snow tires installed. In February, it's the President's Day sales event. For decades, that weekend was massive on the East Coast—from Washington, D.C. to Maine. Now it's not quite what it used to be, but it's still a sta-

CHAPTER EIGHT

ple of the retail automotive calendar. And everywhere you look, dealerships are advertising "best deals," "biggest discounts," and "President's Day Blowouts."

But here's the thing: none of it has a real message. It's all garbled. Everyone's saying the same thing with slightly different graphics and louder music, and none of it connects. None of it differentiates.

What's missing isn't effort. What's missing is *clarity*.

When you don't have a plan, you don't have a foundation to build from. So you default to what everyone else is doing. You use the same sale language, the same seasonal hooks, and the same tired promotions—because at least they're familiar. But familiarity doesn't inspire trust. It doesn't build loyalty. It doesn't help anyone understand why they should choose you over the dozens of other options they're seeing.

There *are* dealerships that do this well, though. One example stands out. There's a Chevrolet dealership in my area that has built a strong, clear message—and it shows up in every commercial. You don't have to guess what they stand for. You don't have to decode the words flying across the screen. The tone is calm, the delivery is warm, and it's consistent.

What makes it even more powerful is who delivers the message. It's not a slick spokesperson. It's not a fast-talking sales executive. It's the dealer's daughter. She might be running the store herself now. Either way, she's not just a figurehead—she's real. She's present. And she speaks like someone who knows the business from the inside.

Every commercial follows a structure. "Here are three reasons to buy from us." Simple. Grounded. Clear. One of those reasons? Total transparency. The prices are right on the windows. You don't have to wonder what something costs—it's there, straightforward and honest.

And it works.

When that dealership speaks, people *understand* them. There's no confusion. No filler. Just a clear, defined message that makes people feel like they know what they're walking into.

That's what planning does. That's what strategy delivers. Not just more advertising, but better communication. Not just noise, but *meaning*.

Marketing isn't about being the loudest voice. It's about being the clearest one.

IN A CROWDED MARKET, DEFINE WHO YOU ARE

Years ago, I worked with a single-point used car store that was struggling with revenue. With one location, they had only one shot at making it work. And for a long stretch, it just didn't.

The store couldn't gain traction. They kept changing the name, trying to figure out what they wanted to be. At one point, they

CHAPTER EIGHT

decided they were going to specialize—two-year-old vehicles coming off lease. That was going to be their thing. But then they ran into legal trouble. Another company had already claimed the name they were using. It wasn't intentional, but it was enough to throw everything off course.

So they pivoted. But instead of sharpening the message, they did the opposite. They moved from being specific to trying to be everything. Every kind of car. Every kind of buyer. They leaned into the idea that if they offered something for everyone, they'd attract more people. But that only works if you have the inventory to back it up. Hundreds of cars. A wide, diverse selection. The kind of scale a national chain could pull off. They were a single-point store. They didn't have that scale.

What they became instead was a mixed bag—trying to appeal to every customer segment at once. At one point, they even dabbled in "buy here, pay here" financing, hoping to catch low-credit buyers. But the result was confusion, not connection. Their identity blurred. Their message disappeared.

One day, just to make a point, I drove five miles north from their location and counted 11 competitors on the same road. Then I drove five miles south—12 more. That's 23 dealerships within ten miles, all competing for the same attention, the same traffic, the same sales.

I brought those numbers back to the table and laid them down. "You're trying to be everything to everybody," I said, "and you can't be. Not like this."

"But we have the biggest inventory," the dealer argued.

"No, you don't," I countered. "Everyone else has the same inventory. If I'm the customer, why would I choose you?"

They couldn't answer that question. Why *would* someone choose them? If their used car lot had the same vehicles as the luxury dealership up the road—places that carried more credibility, stronger branding, better name recognition—what made this place different?

The dealership had even distanced itself from the auto group it belonged to, convinced that the group wasn't well-known enough to make a difference. But without that association, they were just another standalone name on a building that used to belong to a new car franchise. Their identity was unclear. Their value was invisible.

What they needed was a distinct message—something real, something people could latch onto.

An example came to mind. Years ago, just outside Providence, Rhode Island, there was a General Motors dealership known for something very specific. It was an Oldsmobile dealer, but if you were looking for a one- or two-year-old car with low mileage and a better price than new, this was the place you went. Everyone in the area knew it. They branded themselves around that one idea, and it worked. They couldn't keep cars on the lot. They sold out constantly. People lined up for the chance to get in on it.

CHAPTER EIGHT

That was the model. That's what the struggling used car dealership could've done. Something focused. Something memorable. Something that clearly said, "Here's what we do, and here's why it matters."

But they didn't. They dismissed my advice. The message stayed vague. And after over a year of struggling, and losing more than a million dollars, they eventually closed the store.

It's a tough story, but it holds the heart of the lesson: if you don't stand for something specific, you get lost in the noise. Because when customers have dozens of options, they don't need a dealer who claims to do everything. They need one that does *something* with purpose and clarity.

A clear message isn't an afterthought; it's the foundation of what makes people remember you, trust you, and come back to you.

Remember: if you try to be everything to everybody, you end up not being *anything* to *anybody*.

KEY TAKEAWAYS ON MARKETING

Here are five key takeaways from this chapter:

1. **A dealership needs a clear, compelling message.** Without one, it will struggle to stand out, no matter how much it spends on advertising or operations. Clarity in messaging gives both customers and employees something to believe in and align around.

2. **Find your market differentiation.** Most dealerships rely on recycled language and tired promotions that blend into the noise, failing to connect with the market in a meaningful way. Differentiation comes from understanding what the market truly needs and boldly stepping into unmet opportunities.

3. **Effective messaging begins with deep knowledge of your market and your competitors.** Without listening to customers and studying the competitive landscape, it's impossible to identify the gaps that offer real growth potential.

4. **The dealerships that thrive are the ones willing to claim a specific identity.** Even if it means narrowing your focus, a clear message about

CHAPTER EIGHT

what you uniquely offer builds trust, loyalty, and long-term traction in a crowded field.

5. **Trying to be everything to everybody leads to confusion and missed opportunities.** In today's marketplace, the clearest message—not the loudest—wins.

CHAPTER NINE

BEYOND THE ROADMAP: COACHING THROUGHOUT THE ORGANIZATION

Congratulations; you've finished learning the 8-Step Roadmap that will take your dealership from good to great.

However, your work is not done. As a leader, it's natural for you to instill the practices you want to see in your organization and take a strong hand in their implementation. But as the head of the company, you also have a busy job and only so many hours in your already packed day. You can't be everywhere at once, so how do you make sure your employees continue to live the culture, systems, and mindsets that you know will make your dealership thrive?

There's a secret sauce that brings everything you've learned in this book together: building a coaching organization.

In this chapter, you're going to learn the coaching methodology that will turn your company culture into something employees don't just think about, but *live*. This coaching system was first adapted from the Metronomics Coaching Cascade system, and the word "cascade" is what truly makes this system so impactful. Using this chapter, you'll cascade effective coaching from the top of your organization—starting with you, the leader—all the way through every single employee until you have a dealership that runs like a smooth, aligned machine.

A REGULAR COACHING PRACTICE

If you want a dealership culture that people believe in and are proud to be part of then coaching can't be a one-time conversation. It can't be something leaders do only when there's a problem or when someone's performance dips. Coaching has to be regular, structured, and woven into the rhythm of how you work together.

At its core, coaching is about connection. It's a chance to slow down, check in, and say, "I see you. I value your growth here." That kind of message, when delivered consistently, sends a powerful signal about what kind of culture you're building. It says that you don't just care about numbers on a board—you care about people and their potential. And in a dealership, where the pace is fast and the pressure is high, that kind of steady support matters more than ever.

What makes regular coaching so impactful is that it builds trust over time. When employees know they can count on meaningful conversations, not just reactive feedback, they start to open up. They ask more questions. They admit when they're stuck. They take more ownership. Culture grows in those moments. Not from a values poster on the wall, but from the everyday work of showing up for one another.

Coaching isn't just for correcting behavior or fixing mistakes. It's also where we reinforce what's working, celebrate growth, and align people with the dealership's mission and values. Think about a new service advisor who's learning the ropes. If their only feedback comes after something goes wrong, they're not learning—they're bracing for the bad news, always waiting for the hammer to come down. But if they're having regular check-ins where they're encouraged, challenged, and invited into the bigger picture, that's a whole different experience. That's how people grow with confidence instead of fear.

To be effective, coaching must be part of the culture, a normal routine. A structured coaching routine might include weekly or biweekly one-on-ones, a shared agenda, and time carved out for both performance feedback and personal development. I'm going to show you an example of a structured coaching routine that has worked extremely well for the dealerships I've worked with. You're welcome to tweak it to fit the unique needs of your team.

Consistency is key here. If coaching only happens sporadically, it sends the message that development is optional—or worse, that it's only for people who are struggling. But when coaching is consistent across the team, it levels the playing field. It says, "We all have room to grow, and we're committed to doing it together."

In dealerships, where turnover is high and morale can swing quickly, culture has to be reinforced every day. Coaching gives leaders a reliable way to do that. Not with grand speeches or once-a-year surveys, but through steady, honest, human conversations.

START WITH THE WHAT

Coaching starts with the *what*.

It may sound simple, but it's the foundation. Before we can have meaningful conversations with employees about their growth, motivation, or performance, we need to begin with clarity. What are they aiming for? What does success actually look like in their role? Without that shared understanding, coaching quickly turns into guesswork. And when people feel like they're being evaluated without knowing what the target is, trust starts to erode.

Every role in every department should have a clear what: a defined goal they're working toward. This isn't just for salespeople. It's true for advisors, technicians, service managers, parts counter staff—everyone. When the expectations are defined, we create the conditions for fair, supportive, and honest coaching. Without that clarity, even the best coaching intentions fall flat.

To bring this to life, we'll use the example of a salesperson and a forecast spreadsheet. It's an easy way to visualize what we mean

CHAPTER NINE

by the what. A forecast spreadsheet outlines specific targets over a period of time—typically the current month and the next two or three months. It breaks down what the salesperson wants to achieve and the activities that support it. But what makes it so effective is that it doesn't just present an outcome. It connects that outcome to the specific steps required to get there.

If you're reading this and thinking, "We don't do forecasting at our dealership," this is your nudge to go back and reread Chapter Four: Finances. Forecasting isn't optional. It's a core part of building structure around performance. Without it, we're asking people to hit moving targets. That's frustrating for everyone involved.

Knowing where you're going is essential. We would never get in the car for a cross-country trip without a map. And we definitely wouldn't set out without a clear destination. The same is true for coaching. If the employee doesn't know where they're headed, then every conversation becomes reactive—focused only on what went wrong, or what could be better, rather than where we're going and how we'll get there.

Defining the what offers structure, but it also offers direction. It gives you something to point to, something to reflect on, and something to adjust together. When you begin there, you set the tone for a coaching culture that's built on purpose, not pressure.

NEXT: THE WHY

Once you've helped someone identify what they're working toward—whether that's through a forecast spreadsheet, a monthly goal, or a performance target—the next step in coaching is uncovering the *why*. And that's where things really start to shift. Because the "what" gives us structure, but the "why" gives us meaning. That's what brings coaching to life.

Let's say you're sitting down with someone, and they've got their forecast pulled up. You can see their goals laid out in numbers and timelines. That's the roadmap. It shows where they want to go. But now it's time to ask: *Why do you want to get there? What's this goal really about for you?*

This is where coaching moves beyond tactics and into something deeper. One of the most common responses people give when asked about their why is, "Well, I need this number to break even," or "That's what I need to pay my bills." That answer might be honest, but it's not inspiring. Paying your bills is a basic requirement. There's nothing exciting or motivating about keeping the lights on. It's necessary, yes—but it's not what gets people out of bed with energy and purpose.

So, in those moments, the invitation is to go deeper. What else? What's behind that number that matters to you? What do you want that's bigger than breaking even?

CHAPTER NINE

That's where the concept of a *dream inventory* comes in. Some people might call it a bucket list, but the language matters here. "Bucket list" often refers to goals we push far into the future—things we'll get to *someday*. But *dream inventory* keeps it closer. More tangible. These are goals we're working toward in the next 60 to 90 days. The short-term window creates urgency and clarity. It makes the goal feel real. It's not a distant fantasy; it's something you could reach for right now.

When people articulate their short-term dreams, their whole energy shifts. You can see it in their body language, hear it in their voice. A goal tied to a personal dream becomes magnetic. It's not about hitting a number because their manager told them to. It's about earning the down payment for a new apartment, taking their partner on a long-promised weekend trip, or finally having the extra income to sign up for that certification course they've been putting off.

This kind of coaching doesn't just help someone perform better. It connects them to a larger purpose—and that's exactly what culture is built on.

In fact, it ties directly to what we talk about in the first two chapters of this book: leadership's responsibility to create and share a vision that people believe in. If I'm working in an organization and I'm not bought into the vision—if I don't believe in where the company is going or how it plans to get there—then eventually, I'm going to feel a disconnect. And if that disconnect gets too wide,

I may need to go somewhere else. Not out of resentment or failure, but simply because I need to work in a place that supports my why. A place where my personal vision can live alongside the company's.

Culture thrives when everyone can connect their personal why to the organization's bigger mission. When coaching includes these vision-based conversations at the individual level, you're practicing that same leadership concept in real time. You're saying, "Let's talk about what you want. Let's find where that connects to what we're building here together."

When that connection happens—when people feel ownership over their goals, their growth, and the future of the team—that's when culture stops being a statement on a poster and becomes something people live and breathe every day. When people have a hand in shaping the vision, they stop needing to be sold on it and they just start living it.

PUT IT INTO ACTION WITH THE HOW

Once you've nailed down the what and the why, it's time to lay out an action plan for *how* the person you're coaching is going to get it done.

The how brings it all together. Most people can set goals; they've been doing that all their lives. But following through takes structure. It takes a process. The how gives us a practical way to support

CHAPTER NINE

that follow-through.

This is where the coaching process starts to feel like project planning. Think of it like any project you've ever managed. You define the outcome, connect it to a meaningful reason, and then build a plan with steps, timelines, and accountability. The same structure applies here. And it's why you treat the how as more than a motivational prompt. It's a tool for real results.

But before you can even map out the how, there's often a moment in the coaching process when someone says, "I'd love to do this, but I just don't have the time." That's a common response—and it's exactly where I like to use something called The 168 Exercise.

The 168 Exercise begins with one simple fact: there are 168 hours in a week. Most of us never stop to ask how we're actually spending them. So, the first step is to get curious. In the exercise, I break time into three main buckets: sleep, work, and personal development time (or PDT). Sleep and work are usually easy for people to estimate. But personal development? That's where the fog rolls in. Most people aren't sure. They guess. They generalize. And when they add up sleep and work and subtract that from 168, what's left is usually a surprising amount of time that no one can account for.

Next, I ask people to break that leftover time into six categories that make up the personal development section—things like health, relationships, learning, creativity, rest, or community. And that's when real awareness starts to surface. Most people realize they've had more control over their time than they thought. It's not that they *don't* have time to invest in coaching or growth. It's that they haven't seen how they're actually spending their time.

Once we've defined what's happening presently, we move toward the ideal. How many hours would you *like* to spend in each category? What would a balanced week look like? And how does that time investment support your goals?

It's not a complicated exercise, but it's powerful. It makes the invisible visible. It's a lot like sitting down with a financial planner for the first time and realizing you have no idea where your money went—but knowing that now, you want to tell it where to go. The 168 Exercise helps people do the same with their time.

Awareness is often the beginning of change. When people first begin coaching, they might expect tactical advice or strategies for hitting performance goals. And yes, we'll get there. But more often than not, one of the most powerful shifts happens when someone simply sees their time for what it is: a finite, precious resource that—just like money—can be spent with intention or lost without notice.

Think about the first time you tracked a forecast and realized, "We spent *how much* on eating out last month?" There's no shame in it, but there is surprise. And from surprise comes the opening for choice. That's exactly what happens when people begin to track their time with the same honesty and structure they might use to

CHAPTER NINE

track their money.

Time, like money, tells a story. Most of us don't know what story we're telling until we stop and take a look.

The 168 Exercise does just that. It creates a mirror. There are 168 hours in a week, and most people, when asked to estimate how they spend those hours, rely on rough guesses. They know how much they work, roughly. They know how much they sleep, probably. But when asked about personal development time—the hours left over for growth, relationships, health, rest—they often draw a blank.

That's where this exercise becomes more than a worksheet. It becomes a tool for truth-telling. It shows people that while their calendars may feel full, not everything on them is non-negotiable. Sometimes the issue isn't time itself—it's how time is being used.

Now, when someone sees they *do* have a few hours a day that fall into the "personal development" bucket, the next question is: *When, exactly, are those hours happening?* That's where reality sets in. Because maybe those hours overlap with family dinners, commutes, dog walks—activities that might not be traditionally productive but are very much a part of life.

This is where coaching shifts from numbers to habits. When people say, "I still don't have time," it's usually not resistance; it's routine. They're operating on autopilot. Maybe they unwind in front of the TV at night, and it feels essential. And maybe it is. But maybe it's just familiar. The real coaching work is in helping them ask: *Is there another way I could get what I need from that time?*

Could that 30 minutes of downtime come from sitting on the porch with a partner? From walking the dog while listening to an audiobook? From something restorative that also moves them closer to their goals?

The goal isn't to judge how time is spent. It's to shine a light on it. To create enough awareness that people can make choices that feel right *for them*. Because one of the hardest habits to break isn't laziness or procrastination—it's unexamined routine.

Here's an important point: you can't just add more in. If you're already full, something has to come out to make room for something new. That's not failure, it's just reality. Good coaching doesn't try to pretend otherwise. It doesn't say, "Just do more." It says, "Let's make space for what matters most. What are you willing to give up—even temporarily—to get the return you really want?"

Sometimes, yes, that means replacing an hour of rewatching old TV episodes with journaling, or goal planning, or rest. Other times, it means *keeping* that TV time because it's the best way to decompress before meaningful connection with family later in the evening. The point isn't to scrap it all. The point is to *know* what it is—and choose it, rather than drift into it.

In the end, awareness always comes first. It's not about perfect use of time. It's about intentional use of time. And once someone sees their time clearly—once they realize they can reshape it—the change begins. Not because they were told to, but because they

CHAPTER NINE

want to.

THE GOAL ACHIEVEMENT PROCESS WORKSHEET

To create the clearest possible visual roadmap, I use a tool called the Goal Achievement Process Worksheet. It's a structure that brings clarity, emotion, and accountability to the table. When used fully, it shifts the way people approach their goals—whether those goals are personal, professional, or somewhere in between.[3]

The version I use has been around for decades. I didn't create it myself, but I've worked with it for over 25 years, across all types of roles and personalities. I've seen it take on many forms, but the essence stays the same: most people don't take the time to *plan* how they'll achieve a goal. They might write it down or talk about it, but they rarely stop long enough to build a real path to get there.

And that's the difference. When someone finally does walk through the full process, something shifts. You can see it happen. Excitement shows up. So does belief. They begin to visualize success not just as a possibility, but as something real. Of course, discomfort can also surface. They may hit points where they realize, "I might not be able to get around this." That's good. That's where the process earns its value.

---

3 Adapted from the Trusted Advisors Network framework.

One of the most powerful sections in this tool—often the part that people want to skip over—is the section on *rewards and consequences*. If someone sets a goal—let's say, "I want to take my family on a weekend at the lake"—we don't stop there. We ask, "What else will happen when you achieve that?" And again, "What else?" We drill into that four, five, even seven layers deep, until the reward stirs something emotional. Until they feel it in the pit of their stomach. That's when the "why" stops being intellectual and starts being personal.

And we do the same thing with consequences. "What happens if you don't get there?" Again, no one-word answers allowed. We dig. We surface the real pain—not to create guilt, but to create awareness. This part of the process is what makes it stick. When people are emotionally connected to both the benefit of succeeding and the cost of failing, they don't just set goals—they commit to them.

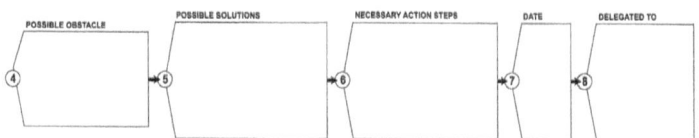

Then we go a step further and talk about *obstacles*. Most people skip this step. They say, "I want to do this," and charge out the door. Thirty days later, they haven't made progress, and they don't know why. But if we do this right, we ask: "What's going to get in

CHAPTER NINE

the way?" We write those down. Then, for every obstacle, we identify possible solutions, the steps that will support those solutions, and who will help us carry them out.

We also add two key details: when the action step starts, and when it ends. That's not just a technicality. Without a clear start date, a lot of well-intentioned steps never begin. So we lock it in: when it begins, when it ends, and who's involved. Even if you're managing the goal yourself, you still identify whether there's someone mentoring or supporting you along the way.

I remember working with a coach once who listed 27 obstacles to one goal. Twenty-seven! He dug deep and got specific. Not everyone will do that, and that's okay. Even identifying two or three obstacles is enough to start. Others will reveal themselves along the way. They always do. The point is to anticipate—not to get stuck in the problems, but to stop being surprised by them.

What makes this whole process powerful is its ability to turn vague intentions into practical commitments. It pushes people past the surface and into action. And that's why I always describe it as life-changing. Once you've used this tool the way it's designed, it's hard to miss a goal, because you've given yourself a map, a reason, and a way through every barrier that might show up.

HOPE IS NOT A STRATEGY

It's easy for dealership owners or department leaders to look at tools like the Dream Inventory or coaching conversations around personal goals and ask, "What does this have to do with business?"

On the surface, it might seem like personal development lives in a separate category from profitability. But the truth is, the connection between the two couldn't be clearer.

When you help someone connect what's happening in their professional life to what they care about personally, you get a better employee. That's not a feel-good theory—it's observable, measurable reality. When people see that success at work can fund the life they want to build, they lean in. They start to care more, give more, and stay longer. They feel invested in something bigger than just the daily grind.

The bottom line is that it works. Not just because it creates clarity, but because it helps people practice something that's foundational to a healthy, high-performing culture: believing in possibility. Too often, employees hear a goal and shut down before they even try. "We'll never hit that number." "That's not realistic." The mindset of *impossibility* is contagious—and it kills momentum.

Helping people think differently about their personal goals trains them to think differently about business goals too. When someone gets used to asking, "What would it take?" instead of "Why won't this work?" in their own life, they bring that same curiosity to the showroom. Instead of rejecting a sales target as unrealistic, they start asking what would need to be true to get there.

In a recent coaching session, I asked a group, "Why don't we

CHAPTER NINE

have anyone consistently selling 30 cars a month?" The room was quiet. The real answer? No one thinks in terms of 30. No one around them is doing it, so it doesn't even seem possible. But what if it is? What if it always was?

In June—a tough month across the board—we still had a few salespeople perform extraordinarily well. The same people who do well month after month, no matter the external conditions. The economy didn't shift for them. The inventory didn't suddenly multiply. What changed? Their mindset. They weren't waiting to see what the month would bring. They were already acting on what was possible.

This is what personal coaching in a professional setting makes room for. It teaches people to separate noise from truth. Yes, there will always be reasons why a customer "shouldn't" buy. Tariffs, interest rates, gas prices—you name it. There will always be something. But people still buy. And someone is always selling.

It's not magic, luck, or hustle alone. It's belief. It's structure. And it's a commitment to not winging it.

Hope is not a strategy. But awareness, intention, and alignment—those are.

THE COACHING CASCADE

Coaching isn't something you can leave to chance. It doesn't just happen because you hire good people or hold weekly meetings.

Coaching is a discipline—it's built on rhythm and structure, not inspiration. And if you want it to reach everyone in the dealership, it has to start at the top and move with intention all the way through their direct supporters.

When I begin this work with a dealership, I always start with the dealer—the person at the very top. That's where the cascade begins. The dealer learns to coach the general managers in a way that fits that level of leadership—high-level, strategic, focused. From there, the general managers are expected to coach their direct supporters: usually the general sales manager and the service manager. Those two then coach the layer below them—sales managers on one side, service advisors on the other. The cascade continues. If we do it right, coaching reaches three, even four layers deep, and every employee in the organization has access to it.

But that's only if we do it right.

When I draw this out on a whiteboard, the gaps show up immediately. It's not the top layer that fails to connect. A general manager sees a salesperson miss a beat and offers feedback on the spot—a quick hallway comment, a shoulder tap, a course correction. All good. But then we look at the layers in between. Who stands beside the mid-level managers? Who's coaching the coaches? Silence.

I've stood in a conference room, surrounded by eight or nine leaders from the dealership, and asked, "On a scale from zero to ten—ten being expert coaching skill, zero being no clue—where

CHAPTER NINE

would you place yourself?" I always say, "We're friends here. No judgment. Say two, say twelve, just be honest." At first, no one moves. So I break it into ranges: zero to two, two to five, five to seven, seven to ten. One hand goes up at the top. One.

Then I ask them to rate the people they're responsible for coaching. The numbers start dropping into the five-to-seven range. We go another layer down, and they fall again. The farther we stretch across the organization, the thinner coaching capacity becomes.

Leadership knows coaching matters, and they can feel the shortage. They see the gap. But what they often don't see is that it's not a time problem—it's a structure problem. Yes, managers are having conversations. Yes, they're checking in. But none of it follows a consistent rhythm or shared approach. So even when they're doing their best, the impact stays scattered.

I once filmed (with permission, of course) three general managers having what they each called a coaching conversation. Same role, same dealership. But their tone, their questions, their follow-through, even their body language—completely different. That kind of inconsistency creates confusion. If we want coaching to feel supportive and strong, not random or reactive, we need shared rituals. We need every leader following the same pattern: same opening move, same flow, same close. When employees experience that consistency, they begin to trust it.

CONSISTENCY + COMMITMENT = CULTURE

As I close this chapter on coaching, there are two final truths worth naming—because they're what allow coaching to actually work, not just in theory, but in practice.

First, the person being coached has to show up prepared. That means taking time before each session to reflect: *How am I doing on the goals I set? What's working? Where am I stuck? What's changed since last time?* Without that reflection, coaching can't go deeper than surface-level status updates. But when someone comes in having already thought through their own progress, the conversation can move straight into insight, strategy, and support. That's where the growth happens. Coaching time is too valuable to spend reviewing information that could've been processed in advance. The real power is in the *conversation*—in the moment we get to ask the hard questions, challenge assumptions, and celebrate meaningful wins.

Second, coaching time itself must be treated as non-negotiable. Whether you're leading the session or receiving support, it needs to be part of your role—not extra, not optional, not "if there's time." When we treat coaching like a luxury or an afterthought, we signal that growth is secondary. But when coaching is part of the rhythm of how we lead, manage, and develop people, it becomes one of the

CHAPTER NINE

clearest ways we reinforce our culture.

Culture isn't built by accident. It's shaped every day by the conversations we make space for—and the ones we don't. A dealership that prioritizes coaching builds more than performance. It builds trust, accountability, resilience, and pride. But that only happens when coaching isn't just something we believe in—it's something we *practice*, consistently, at every level of the organization.

That's the invitation: build the time in, show up ready, and make coaching a shared responsibility. The time you spend doing so will show up in countless ways in the years to come as you build a flourishing dealership that lasts.

KEY TAKEAWAYS ON COACHING

Here are five key takeaways from this chapter:

1. **Coaching must be consistent and routine.** When coaching becomes a structured part of how a dealership operates—not just a reactive measure—it reinforces values, supports growth, and helps build a culture that lasts.

2. **Clear goals create a strong foundation.** Every role needs a defined "what" to aim for, and tools like forecast spreadsheets bring that clarity into focus so that coaching has direction

and purpose.

3. **Personal motivation fuels commitment.** Using tools like the Dream Inventory, employees can connect their goals to something meaningful in their own lives, which deepens engagement and builds lasting alignment with the dealership's mission.

4. **Structure turns intention into action.** The "how" of coaching helps individuals anticipate obstacles, build realistic plans, and use their time with more intention—supported by tools like the 168 Exercise.

5. **Coaching must reach every level of the dealership.** By cascading a shared coaching structure throughout the organization, every employee receives support, creating consistency, accountability, and a deeply rooted culture.

CONCLUSION

If you've made it to the end of this book, I already know something about you.

You're not someone who settles for "good enough." You didn't pick up *The Dealership Manifesto* because you were looking for a couple of quick tips to boost next month's numbers. You're here because you want to build something that lasts. You want a dealership that reflects your values, your leadership, and the standard of excellence you believe in.

The dealership business has never been easy, and it's not meant to be. The truth is that most dealerships don't fail because of the market or the economy. They fail because the work on the inside isn't strong enough. Leadership teams drift out of alignment. Culture becomes something written on a wall instead of lived by the people. Old habits take over while the systems that create real, intentional growth never get put in place.

I've seen that story repeat itself many times. But I've also seen what happens when a leader makes a different choice. When someone decides they're done settling, they pull their team together and commit to creating a dealership built on clarity, discipline, and purpose. The change is never immediate. It builds over time. And if the leader stays consistent, the results always follow.

Here's the part that matters most: no consultant or manufacturer can do this work for you. No playbook can take your place.

This is *your* business, *your* culture, and *your* people.

If you want a dealership that grows with excellence, you have to be the one to start the change. You have to model the behaviors you want to see. You have to set clear expectations and establish the rhythms that keep everyone moving together. You have to be willing to have hard conversations and stay consistent when it'd be easier to let things slide. Leadership matters most in the moments when no one else is watching.

Even though this work is yours to lead, you don't have to carry it alone. Surround yourself with a leadership team that truly shares your vision. Involve your frontline team members, because they see where the gaps are before anyone else. Seek out peers who'll challenge your thinking and hold you accountable. The work is hard, but it was never meant to happen in isolation.

The Dealership Manifesto is a mirror that reflects where you are right now, and it invites you to imagine what's possible for the future. The real question is whether you're willing to do the work that bridges the gap between the two.

If you are, here's what you can expect.

- You'll create a dealership that doesn't just ride out market changes but thrives in the middle of them.

CONCLUSION

- You'll build a team that takes real ownership because they want to, not because they're told to.
- You'll stand out in a crowded market through clarity and excellence, not through gimmicks or noise.
- You'll feel proud of what you've built. It'll be more than a business. It'll be a legacy.

Thank you for taking this journey. The dealership world is full of noise and distractions, but leaders like you are the ones who rise above it.

Now it's time to get to work!

PUTTING THIS BOOK INTO ACTION

In this book, you haven't just learned about fixing broken processes or chasing sales targets. You've also learned about redefining what it means to lead, operate, and grow a dealership in today's business world. You've probably noticed that woven into every chapter is a clear message: *culture isn't an initiative*. It's the operating system of your dealership. It lives in every conversation, every process, every leadership choice, and every customer interaction. Without it, no strategy, process, or promotion will ever create lasting success.

Every department has to function as a connected business unit rather than a silo. In order to do so, your first step is to reinforce to your department leaders that culture isn't a poster on the wall;

it's something they need to model, coach, and execute every day.

Remember these key takeaways as you put this book into action:

- Having the right leaders in the right roles doing the right things comes before anything else.
- Strategy starts with culture.
- Employee experience is the foundation of customer loyalty.
- Cash flow isn't just an accounting task; it's the oxygen of your business.
- Systems have to be documented, aligned, and lived out in practice.
- Execution routines turn intentions into measurable results.
- Your message has to be clear, bold, and differentiated if you want to own your market.
- Coaching is the bridge between culture and consistent performance.

The Dealership Manifesto isn't meant to sit on a shelf. It's meant to be lived, implemented, and shared. If what you've read here resonates with you, the next step is simple—but not easy.

Take Action.

You don't have to do it in isolation; if you're serious about transforming your dealership and want to connect with other growth-minded leaders who are doing the same work, I want to hear from you. Whether it's a candid conversation about where you're stuck, a leadership workshop for your team, or joining a

CONCLUSION

network of dealership owners who are committed to operational excellence, there's a next step for you on the other side of a conversation with me.

Visit thedealershipmanifesto.com for resources designed specifically for dealership leaders who are ready to scale with The 8-Step Dealership Roadmap.

The dealerships that will win the next decade aren't those with the flashiest showroom or the biggest ad spend. They're the ones who commit to being relentlessly disciplined, culturally aligned, and strategically agile.

This is your call to action. You have the blueprint. Now go build it.

GET YOUR SCORE

Start your journey on the 8-Step Roadmap right now by completing the Dealership Manifesto Leadership Scorecard on the following page.

To download a print version of the Scorecard, visit thedealershipmanifesto.com or use the QR code below.

DEALERSHIP MANIFESTO LEADERSHIP SCORECARD

How aligned is your dealership to the 8-Step Roadmap? Use this scorecard to assess where you stand today. Be honest. This is your starting point.

Rate each statement on a scale of 1 to 5:
1 = Strongly Disagree | 3 = Neutral | 5 = Strongly Agree

1. **Leadership Alignment**

- Our leadership team is aligned around a shared vision, mission, and values.

- Every leader understands their role in building culture, not just hitting numbers.

- Leaders are promoted based on capability and alignment, not tenure.

- We do not tolerate misaligned leaders who resist growth, coaching, or accountability.

2. **Cultural Clarity**

- Our culture is defined in clear, actionable terms that guide daily behavior.

- Employees experience our culture through

leadership behavior—not just slogans.

- Coaching is a routine, structured part of how we lead, not a reaction to problems.
- Every employee understands how their role impacts customer experience and company success.

3. Operational Excellence

- We have documented systems and SOPs for all critical processes.
- Departments operate like individual businesses but follow shared principles.
- Cash flow awareness is embedded in leadership conversations, not just finance meetings.
- Forecasting is proactive and data-driven—not reliant on historical habits.

4. Execution Rhythm

- We have daily huddles or meetings that reinforce focus, alignment, and accountability.
- Leaders consistently coach their teams through roleplays, feedback, and real-time guidance.
- Problem-solving routines are in place to ensure

small issues don't become major breakdowns.

- Our team is disciplined in follow-through—we do what we say we'll do.

5. Market Position & Message

- Our dealership has a clear, differentiated message that resonates internally and externally.
- We don't rely on generic promotions; our marketing reflects who we are and why we're different.
- We focus on building long-term customer relationships, not just generating leads.
- Everyone in our dealership—from sales to service—understands their role in delivering our brand promise.

Scoring:

80 - 100: You are leading a dealership that is aligned, intentional, and positioned for sustainable growth. Keep refining your systems and scaling your culture.

60 - 79: You have a solid foundation but critical gaps are holding you back. Prioritize leadership

CONCLUSION

alignment and operational execution rhythms.

40 - 59: Your dealership has foundational misalignments in culture, leadership, and systems. Focus on alignment before chasing growth.

Below 40: You're at risk of constant firefighting, fragmentation, and stagnation. Immediate leadership recalibration is essential.

Your score isn't a judgment. It's a reflection of where you are—and a guide for where to focus next.

ACKNOWLEDGMENTS

Writing this book has been both a humbling and inspiring journey, one that would not have been possible without the guidance, encouragement, and generosity of so many remarkable individuals and organizations.

I am deeply grateful to the Trusted Advisors Network, whose wisdom and community have provided me with a strong foundation of support throughout my professional journey. The collaboration and insight from my colleagues at Gravitas Impact Premium Coaches and the game-changing frameworks of Metronomics have also been invaluable in shaping the ideas and practices presented in these pages.

Special thanks go to David Herdlinger, Doug Brown, Tammy Kohl, Wendy Howland, Keith Cupp, Shannon Susko, and Meghan McCracken whose thought leadership, coaching, friendship, and personal encouragement have left a lasting mark on both my work and my life.

I am also profoundly appreciative of the ProActive™ Leadership Group team—Mike Mirau, Julie Poland, Nancy Batterman, and Darren Gardner. Your shared commitment to building better leaders and stronger organizations has been a constant source of motivation and inspiration.

To each of you: thank you for walking alongside me on this journey, challenging me to grow, and reminding me of the extraordinary impact that can be achieved when great minds come together in service of others.

ABOUT THE AUTHOR

Bill Napolitano is a nationally recognized business strategist with a proven track record of helping growth-minded CEOs and their leadership teams overcome the biggest barriers to scaling their organizations. As President and Founder of The Institute for Business Excellence® and a Partner at ProActive™ Leadership Group, Bill specializes in dealership operations across the automotive, motorcycle, powersports, and marine industries, as well as professional and trade services.

He is known for his work in leadership development, talent systems, strategic execution, and cash flow optimization—equipping businesses with the tools to attract top talent, implement disciplined systems, and generate the cash needed for sustainable growth. Bill has earned certifications with Trusted Advisor Network, Scaling Up, Gravitas Impact Premium Coaches, and Metronomics, among many other professional certifications.

A respected speaker, coach, and co-author of *The Real Power of Leadership and Influence,* Bill also serves as a volunteer, faith leader, and proud member of multiple dealership and business associations throughout New England.

www.ingramcontent.com/pod-product-compliance
Lightning Source LLC
Chambersburg PA
CBHW030242010526
44107CB00030B/1300/J